MAX-PLANCK-GESELLSCHAFT

Universität
Augsburg
University

TECHNISCHE
UNIVERSITÄT
MÜNCHEN

THE GEORGE
WASHINGTON
UNIVERSITY

WASHINGTON, DC

MIPLC Studies
Edited by

Prof. Dr. Christoph Ann, LL.M. (Duke Univ.)
TUM School of Management

Prof. Robert Brauneis
The George Washington University Law School

Prof. Dr. Josef Drexl, LL.M. (Berkeley)
Max Planck Institute for Innovation and Competition

Prof. Dr. Michael Kort
University of Augsburg

Prof. Dr. Thomas M.J. Möllers
University of Augsburg

Prof. Dr. Dres. h.c. Joseph Straus
Max Planck Institute for Innovation and Competition

Volume 30

Guangjie Li

Revisiting China's Competition Law and Its Interaction with Intellectual Property Rights

Nomos

MIPLC Munich   Augsburg
       Intellectual München
       Property   Washington DC
       Law Center

The Deutsche Nationalbibliothek lists this publication in the
Deutsche Nationalbibliografie; detailed bibliographic data
are available on the Internet at http://dnb.d-nb.de

a.t.: Munich, Master Thesis Munich Intellectual Property Law Center, 2017

ISBN   978-3-8487-5018-4 (Print)
         978-3-8452-9268-7 (ePDF)

British Library Cataloguing-in-Publication Data
A catalogue record for this book is available from the British Library.

ISBN   978-3-8487-5018-4 (Print)
         978-3-8452-9268-7 (ePDF)

Library of Congress Cataloging-in-Publication Data
Li, Guangjie
Revisiting China's Competition Law and Its Interaction with Intellectual Property
Rights
Guangjie Li
79 p.
Includes bibliographic references.

ISBN   978-3-8487-5018-4 (Print)
         978-3-8452-9268-7 (ePDF)

1st Edition 2018
© Nomos Verlagsgesellschaft, Baden-Baden, Germany 2018. Printed and bound in Germany.

Foreword

With the interplay between competition law and IP rights becoming ever more intense in major economies a functioning framework is required to discourage monopolistic behaviour while stimulating innovation and consumer protection.

In this dissertation the author studies issues at the nexus between China's Anti-Monopoly Law (AML) and a fast-evolving IP regime. *De jure* the two legal systems pursue coherent goals of attaining maximum efficiencies in society and enhancing consumer welfare. *De facto* the aims are achieved through seemingly opposite means, i.e. safeguarding free competition for all market players versus granting exclusive rights to IP owners. Competition authorities and judicial bodies face immense challenges as they attempt to strike an optimal balance between the two regimes.

The history of the US and German competition policies which are touched upon in this paper highlights the impact of the socio-economic environment on judicial and administrative decisions. In view of the evolving requirements of competition regime within the boundaries of sovereign states, readers are encouraged to adopt a holistic view when examining the Chinese competition policy. The dynamics of China's competition law and its interrelationship with IP rights is clearly mirrored in recent administrative and court decisions. Though strongly aligned to international rules and doctrines, the latest *Anti-Monopoly Guidelines on the Abuse of Intellectual Property Rights* (IP Guidelines) released by the Chinese authorities reflect the leadership's determination to upgrade technological standards by actively promoting high-tech industries and pushing for indigenous innovation as a driving force for sustainable economic development.

Having joined the ranks of the world's leading IP jurisdictions, China has been constantly improving its legal framework to protect the interest of IP owners. At the time of submitting the thesis (September 2017), there were three specialized IP courts and four newly-established IP tribunals in China. By March 1, 2018 the number of specialized IP tribunals had increased to 15. On March 13, 2018 a reform plan was submitted to the 13th National People's Congress for deliberation. The idea is to consolidate the scattered Chinese IP institutions into one single body, which would be responsible for all IP matters including patents, trademarks, copyrights and geographical indications. The aim of the reform is, *inter alia*, to unify standards and to effectively enforce IP rights.

August 1, 2018 will mark the tenth anniversary of the enactment of China's AML. The introduction of the competition law reflects China's successful transition from a centrally-planned to a market economy. In turn, effective enforcement of competition policies contributes to the enhancement of a free market economy and the increase of consumer welfare. Despite being a relatively young jurisdiction, China's successful adoption of the AML and its careful formulation of the *IP Guidelines* may serve as an example for other emerging economies on the verge of moving in a similar direction.

April 30, 2018   *Guangjie Li*

Table of Contents

Abstract

China is rapidly moving in the direction of a market-based economy. Consequently, its legal system is continuously adjusted and modernized. This thesis elaborates on latest developments and efforts by the Chinese authorities to bring the country's competition law and its enforcement mechanisms in line with international standards. It also describes the interdependence and mutual impregnation between competition law and intellectual property rights, two aspects which will greatly impact corporate behaviour.

The basic goal of competition law is to protect competition processes in the economy by regulating monopolistic conduct of market participants. The driving force behind a healthy rivalry between companies is to achieve higher sales and profits, and to stimulate new ideas while guaranteeing consumers that they receive the best possible offer in terms of technology and price. Innovation and creativity will give companies the technical advantages required to achieve good performance and eventually market leading positions. In order to overcome market failure and to protect innovators from "free-riders" of intellectual property and make it possible for them to recover their investments, IP regime confers innovators exclusive rights in a given jurisdiction for a certain period of time.

Both competition law and an effective IPR regime are essential to promote and maintain competitive market structures. "Excessive" exercise of IPRs can lead to market distortion, while overly enforcement against IPR holders will discourage innovation. The interaction between these two regimes is a hotly debated topic among scholars, the legal profession and industrial players. Such discussions are heated up depending on different perceptions and viewpoints of fair competition.

Modern competition law evolved within the national boundaries of sovereign states. Country specific features in particular socio-economic and political aspects influence the design of the law and its legal and public enforcement institutions. Numerous judicial and administrative decisions from major jurisdictions such as the US and the EU demonstrated that primary goals of competition law can have a different emphasis and evolve over time. This illustrates the dynamics of competition law, which must be viewed in the context of a country's history and tradition.

Acronyms and Abbreviations

AMC	Anti-Monopoly Commission
AMEA	Anti-Monopoly Enforcement Agencies
AML	Anti-Monopoly Law
Art.	Article
AUCL	Anti-Unfair Competition Law
BRICS	Brazil, Russia, India, China, South Africa
DOJ	Department of Justice
ECJ	European Court of Justice
EPO	European Patent Office
ETSI	European Telecommunications Standardisation Institute
EU	European Union
FRAND	Fair, reasonable, and non-discrimination
FTC	Federal Trade Commission
GDP	Gross domestic product
IC	International Competition Network
IDC	InterDigital Technology Corporation, Inc.
IP	Intellectual property
IPR	Intellectual property right
ITC	US International Trade Commission
JFTC	Japan Fair Trade Commission
JV	Joint venture
KFTC	Korean Fair Trade Commission
MOFCOM	Ministry of Commerce
NDRC	National Development and Reform Commission
NPC	National People's Congress
PRC	People's Republic of China
R&D	Research & Development
SAIC	State Administration of Industry and Commerce
SASAC	State-owned Assets Supervision and Administration Commission
SEP	Standard essential patent
SETC	State Economic & Trade Commission
SIPO	State Intellectual Property Office
SOE	State-owned enterprise
SPC	Supreme People's Court
SSO	Standard setting organisation
TFEU	Treaty on the Functioning of the European Union
TRIPS	Agreement on Trade-Related Aspects of Intellectual Property Rights
TTBER	Technology Transfer Block Exemption Regulation
WTO	World Trade Organisation

I. Introduction: China's Successful Journey Toward A Modern Judicial System

A. China's Socio-Economic Progress

Since the launch of the economic reform policy in 1978, China has experienced a period of more than thirty years of successful economic development. During the transitional period from a planned economy to a market-based economy, China has designed a series of industrial policies to encourage the fast development of its economy by promoting foreign direct investment, importing advanced foreign technologies and promoting exports. Meanwhile, China has become the second biggest economic power in the world in terms of GDP, just after the United States.

Even if it is debatable in the international community that China is a market economy, what should not be ignored, however, is the vital role private companies play in the Chinese national economy. According to the statistics released by the State Administration of Taxation (SAT) that Chinese private sector generated almost 70 percent of the GDP in 2016. In the same year more than 50 percent of tax revenue was contributed by privately-owned enterprises, which also provided more than 80 percent of employment opportunities in the country.[1]

Nowadays, legislative framework makes Chinese state-owned enterprises (SOEs) directly exposed to competition with newly emerged private companies from home and abroad. This is especially true after China joined WTO in 2001. Thanks to the economic transformation, China has lifted 800 million people out of poverty since 1978. Today, the government has a new, ambitious goal of lifting all 55 million extremely poor citizens out of poverty by 2020.[2] All these achievements are due to, among others, efficient market economy through the introduction of a series competition laws in China: Price law, Anti-Unfair Competition Law,

---

1 Press release from *Daily Economic News* (每日经济新闻), April 6, 2017, available at http://www.sohu.com/a/132323997_701102?_f=v 2-index-feeds.
2 The world Bank: *Understanding China's Poverty Reduction Success to Benefit the Global South,* available at http://www.worldbank.org/en/news/feature/2016/05/17/understanding-chinas-poverty-reduction-success-to-benefit-the-global-south

Consumer Protection Law, and preeminently, the introduction of Anti-Monopoly Law (AML). As stated in Art. 1 of the AML, the purpose of the law is "raising economic efficiency, safeguarding the interests of consumers."

B. Origins of China's Anti-Monopoly Law

Competition policy and relevant guidelines in China are not entirely new, although they were "closely integrated with industrial policies and deviate from modern antitrust laws adopted in other advanced economies"[3]. However, only as late as 2007 was the first Chinese Anti-Monopoly Law (AML) promulgated, after going through thirteen years of debate and three revisions. It finally came into effect on August 1, 2008.[4] The long delay of the adoption of the AML was no secret: The Chinese government needed to implement strategic plans to encourage the development of its domestic industry in several key sectors which stood in conflict with some of the goals set by the AML.[5] To a large extent, various foreign multinational investors as well as large Chinese SOEs exploited the *legislative vacuum* during that period of time by forming conglomerates.[6]

---

3 Huyue Zhang, *An Economic Analysis of China's Anti-Monopoly Law,* (ProQuest LLC, 2011) 20.

4 Guangjie Li, *Interface between International Property Rights and Competition Law - Implications of the Chinese Qualcomm Decision (2015),* Seminar Paper submitted to Prof. Josef Drexl on April 15, 2017.

5 *Id.*

6 Precisely due to the fear of potential damages the AML law may cause to foreign investors and also to Chinese SOEs alike, the AML of China underwent such a long period of debate. However, examples of acquisition of Chinese leading companies in various industries by large multi-national corporations demonstrated evident harm caused to Chinese national industries as well consumer sectors, which was often caused by insufficient control or inefficient approval procedures on mergers & acquisition (M&A) deals. For instance, the French company Danone has actively acquired majority shares of Chinese dairy food companies since 1987 (e.g. Wuhan Brewery with 54.2% shares, Shenzhen Yili Food Company with 54.2% shares). In 2000 Danone acquired 92% shares of Lebaishi Group (Information available at http://www.360doc.com/content/16/0522/20/8536324_561406743.shtml). Participation of foreign players brought factually higher quality of products. However, dominant positions in relevant product markets also led to excessively high prices that Chinese consumers had to bear.

Since the adoption of the AML the international community has been observing closely how the Chinese anti-monopoly enforcement agencies (AMEAs) as well as the judiciary system put the legislation into practice. Some commentators expressed their concerns about possible biased attitude of the AMEAs against foreign companies. Very often each decision regarding foreign players tends to be taken with a second guess. However, it turned out that the AMEAs have been active at issuing decisions against both Chinese and foreign companies for their anticompetitive conduct. The quality of AMEAs' decisions and court judgements keeps improving. Though a newcomer in this field, China has established itself as one of the major jurisdictions for competition issues in the world through a series of landmark decisions issued by both administrative and judicial bodies in recent years.

In 2011, the National Development and Reform Commission (NDRC) commenced investigations into two Chinese telecom giants, *China Telecom* and *China Unicom* for abuse of dominant market position. The investigations focused on refusal to deal and price discrimination, which resulted in many internet service providers being forced out of the market. The two telecom giants had to undertake rectifications, including increasing internet speeds and decreasing internet fees. In 2015 the NDRC issued a landmark decision on *Qualcomm* with the highest penalty (almost USD 1 billion) ever imposed on a single company based on *Qualcomm's* abuse of its dominant market position and charging excessive royalty fees for its standard essential patents (SEPs). This decision attracted great attention in the world. In November 2016, against the Swiss company *Tetra Pak* the State Administration of Industry and Commerce (SAIC) issued the lengthiest administrative decision ever released by a Chinese competition enforcement agency. The decision analysed in detail the market definition, identification of a dominant position and also provided detailed assessment of the abusive conduct of *Tetra Pak*.

Apart from administrative decisions, private actions filed at competent courts based on Art. 50[7] of the AML have also increased steadily in recent years, particularly after release of the *Provision on the Application of Laws in Civil Disputes Cases Arising from Monopoly Activities* by the Supreme People's Court (SPC) in May 2012. The trend shows that more

---

7 Art. 50 stipulates "Business operators which implement monopoly acts and causing other to suffer losses therefrom shall bear civil liability pursuant to the law".

undertakings and individuals are confident to let courts decide on their claims for losses suffered from violation of competitive law. In June 2016, *Qualcomm* filed law suits against Chinese mobile phone manufacturer *Meizu* for infringing its SEPs, and claiming damages in the amount of RMB 520 million.[8]

The desire to introduce a modern competition law came from within the country in the midst of economic reforms, when the private sector was playing an increasingly important role in the economy. However, the formulation and adoption of the AML is to a certain extent an international "product". During the drafting process of the AML, Chinese government consulted numerous foreign legal and economic experts from the European Union (EU) and the United States (US). Many foreign competition law experts were even directly involved in the drafting of the AML. Leading scholars for competition law from Germany such as Professor Jürgen Basedow of the Max Planck Institute for Comparative and International Private Law and Professor Josef Drexl of the Max Planck Institute for Intellectual Property and Competition Law, and experts from other countries were invited by the State Council Legislative Affairs Office to discuss the draft of the AML.[9]

The AML, enacted in 2008 adopted the modern "three pillar" system and prohibits monopolistic conduct in the following areas:
- Monopoly agreements between business operators (Chapter II)
- Abuse of dominant market position by business operators (Chapter III)
- Concentration of business operators which may have the effect of eliminating competition (Chapter IV).

Owing to China's legacy of a planned economy and its state-owned enterprises (SOEs), Chapter V of the AML prohibits the abuse of administrative powers for elimination or restriction of competition.[10]

---

8 *Qualcomm Sued Meizu, Claiming Damages of RMB 520 Million* (高通起诉魅族侵权案详情：索赔 5.2 亿元) Available at http://news.mydrivers.com/1/488/488454.htm.

9 Xiaoye Wang, "*China's Competition Law in the Global Competition*" in Nicolas Charbit, Elisa Ramundo (eds.), *Competition Law on the Global Stage: David Gerber's Global Competition Law in Perspective*, Institute of Competition Law (2014).

10 Chapter V of the AML addresses the role of Chinese administrative authorities, given the history of planned economy and specific characteristic of the Chinese socialist market economy.

The adoption of the AML will definitely make China more committed to the mechanism of a market economy. And free competition will, in turn, make Chinese companies more performing. The aggregate efficiency will greatly benefit consumer interests. After epochal above-average growth China is in many cases not a cheap production site any more. In our knowledge-based world, innovation and advanced technology are powerful weapons to make companies superior to their competitors. The emergence of numerous high-tech companies and national champions such as *Huawei, ZTE, Haier, Alibaba, Tencent* and other start-up companies in various industrial sectors makes legal protection of intellectual property (IP) essential, also in the context of a globalized world economy.[11]

C. *Origins of China's Patent Law*

In 1984 the first Patent Law of the People's Republic China was promulgated; it entered into force on April 1, 1985. With the help of European, mainly German IP experts, the first draft of the China Patent Law was more or less an "imported" legislation in consideration of the Chinese social, political and economic environment at that time. Since then Chinese Patent Law has gone through three revisions; the fourth amendment of the patent law is currently under consultation.

Similar to the competition regime, the IPR system in China has experienced a process of improvement and adaptations to international standards. The process of adopting global norms was, to a certain extent, driven by international political and economic pressure. The first revision of the Chinese Patent Law in 1992 was more or less an exchange for better trading terms with the US government during the Sino-US trade negotiations. The US government demanded China to amend its patent law by adding protection of chemical and pharmaceutical products. Further commitment from the Chinese government was to revise its Copyright Law and to promulgate laws to protect trade secrets.[12]

---

11 *Supra* note 4.
12 Bonan Lin, Jon Wood, Soonhee Jang, *Overview of Chinese Patent Law*, 35th International Congress of the PIPA in Japan, 2004. The Sino-US Trade negotiations started in 1989 and dragged on for two years without real breakthrough, until the US government threatened to put China on the Special 301 blacklist with trade sanctions.

The second amendment of Chinese Patent Law was being carried out during the rounds of negations to become a member of the World Trade Organisation (WTO). Before it successfully joined the WTO, China had to commit itself to reviewing and revising its patent law in order to comply with the *Agreement on Trade-Related Aspects of Intellectual Property Rights* (TRIPS Agreement). Prior to the amendment, Art. 62 of the Chinese Patent Law provided a "non-infringement" exemption, which stipulated that the act of use or sale of a patented product *without knowing the fact* that the product was produced and sold without the permission of the patent proprietor was not an act of infringement. This made it almost impossible for the patentee to effectively stop infringement acts in China. In the revised Patent Law this exemption of "use or sale" without knowledge was deleted from the non-infringing acts[13]. Furthermore, preliminary injunction was for the very first time introduced into the revised Chinese Patent Law. Other amendments such as permissibility to appeal decisions to the court on the validity of utility models and designs from Patent Re-Examination Board (PRB), methods for calculating damages were also adopted in compliance with the requirements of the TRIPS Agreement.[14]

The first two revisions of the Chinese Patent Law illustrated how the intellectual property right (IPR) policy in developing economies can be shaped by developed countries and international treaties. With the Chinese Trademark Law, Copyright Law, and Regulation on the Protection of New Varieties of Plants, and other regulations on the protection of layout-designs of integrated circuits, and for computer software, China has adopted international norms and harmonised its legal system with rest of the world in the area of IPRs.

China is a very young jurisdiction comparing with the IPR system in the EU, the US and some other countries. Yet, due to its global economic power and numerous national champions China has become one of the most important countries for IP matters in the world.[15] In 2017 the China State Intellectual Property Office (SIPO) received more than 1.38 million patent applications; it ranked No. 1 in the world in the seventh consecutive year. [16]

---

13 *Id.*

14 *Id.*

15 *Supra* note 4.

16 Information is available at http://www.sipo.gov.cn/zscqgz/1123516.htm.

The Chinese government realized that quantity of applications is not sufficient. In its 13th Five-Year Plan (2016 – 2020) China put that *innovation* should be the driving force for economic development.[17] Pertinent policy is to move up in the value chain by abandoning old heavy industry and building up high-tech industries.

In the same year when the AML was promulgated, China announced the "Outline of National IP Strategy" *(IP Strategy)*, which set a roadmap for China to become a country of advanced IP creation, utilization and protection by 2020. In its *IP Strategy* China committed itself to carrying out a number of judicial reforms to strengthen the protection of IP rights. One of the major issues was to establish specialized IP Courts in Beijing, Shanghai and Guangzhou, which were officially opened in late 2014. These IP Courts are designed to try cases involving patents, technical secrets, computer software, integrated circuit layout designs, new plant varieties, and cases regarding recognition of well-known trademarks and antitrust issues. As commentators noted, the establishment of specialized IP courts is a milestone of China's recent efforts in improving the IP protection. Early 2017 four new specialized IP Tribunals were established in other four cities in China: Nanjing, Suzhou, Chengdu and Wuhan. By March 1, 2018 the number of IP tribunals had increased to totally 15 in China.[18]

Furthermore, it is noteworthy that damages awarded by the specialized IP Courts have grown continuously in the past years. According to statistics from the Beijing IP Court in 2016, the average amount of damages granted by the Beijing IP Court is RMB 1.41 million (approximately USD 210 000) for patent infringement, comparing with the average damages of RMB 450 000 (USD 68 000) for patent infringement in 2015. On December 6, 2016, the Beijing IP Court issued an unprecedented damage award of RMB 49 million (approx. USD 7.1 million) in favor of the patent holder[19]. This is another signal to demonstrate that Chinese government is de-

---

17 In each of its Five-Year Plan Chinese government outlines its major national strategy, clarifying focusing area of its work, mapping strategies for economic development, setting growth targets.

18 Information is available at http://www.360doc.com/content/18/0505/23/52632151_751462422.shtml.

19 *Watchdata System v. Hengbao Company, Ltd.* (2015) Jing Zhi Min Chu Zi No.441 (2015) (京知民初字第 441 号, 握奇公司诉恒宝公司侵犯发明专利权纠纷案判决书), available at http://www.ciplawyer.cn/article1.asp?articleid=20552&page=3.

termined to punish IPR infringers and further strengthen IP protection in China.

D. Interaction between Competition Policy and Intellectual Property Law

1. Coherent goals of the two systems

As we can see from the above, IPR regime and competition law have evolved as two different systems. However, both systems possess coherent goals. Competition policy seeks to guarantee healthy rivalry among competitors by limiting all kinds of monopolistic behavior at the market. Competition law is the foundation of market economy so that all market participants could benefit an open and level playing field. Free competition can maximize allocative efficiency in society for the benefit of consumers.

The objective of the IPR system is to protect intellectual creations and incentivize inventions and innovations in the society. It grants IPR holders exclusive rights for their innovation for a limited period of time. During this limited period of time the IPR holder has the exclusive power to control the market price, which is usually much higher than his marginal costs. The deadweight loss caused by monopolistic pricing is a distortion of free market competition. However, this will give creators the opportunity to recoup their investment on innovation. The IPR regime is meant to promote innovation for the diffusion of knowledge, for better varieties of products at a cheaper price due to more efficient production methods, thereby enhancing consumer welfare. Notwithstanding, the IPR regime limits competition and it could be regarded as a sort of compromise to balance public and private interests.

2. Possible conflicts between the two systems

Competition law and the IPR regime pursue the same goals but through completely different mechanism. The former is to guarantee fair market competition by prohibiting monopolistic conduct, while the latter grants IPR owners exclusive rights in order to ensure competition at a higher level. There is a general perception that these two policies have inherent conflicts. It should be stated that monopoly is not *per se* anti-competitive; only the abuse of monopolistic market power is regarded as anti-competitive. This principle also applies to IPR holders.

In theory, the general principle between the two regimes is readily understandable. But in practice it is not easy to apply competition law to intellectual property rights. Competition agencies and judiciary bodies have a difficult task to strike the right balance between these two regimes. Overly extensive competition enforcement on IPR holders may hamper innovation; while abuse of IP rights will hinder healthy competition and thus consumer interests. For instance, to balance *ex ante* and *ex post* efficiencies for dynamic economic sectors such as telecommunication and Internet is an extraordinarily difficult task, because many unpredictable factors need to be taken into consideration. This requires, *inter alia*, involvement of sound economic analytical appraisal. In case the negative effect of exercise of exclusive IPR is much bigger than the benefit of overall public interest, compulsory license needs to be imposed on the IPR holders.

Besides complex technologies, the globalized economy keeps on influencing national competition decisions. Above all, competition law systems can never be regarded as an isolated legal instrument. Depending on the socio-economic conditions and different stages of economic development, administrative and judicial decisions also tend to evolve. This phenomenon does not only apply to developing countries, but also to more "mature" jurisdictions such as EU and US. Reconciliation of these two legal systems represents a formidable task for competition agencies and jurisprudence alike.

Since the enactment of China's AML in 2008, almost ten years have passed. Chinese competition agencies have been absorbing experience and knowhow from older jurisdictions, and making efforts to develop guidelines for defining the boundaries between competition law and the intellectual property regime. On March 23, 2017, the very first comprehensive draft IP guidelines *"Anti-Monopoly Guidelines on the Abuse of Intellectual Property Rights"* under the auspice of Anti-Monopoly Commission (AMC) of the State Council was published. The international community is watching closely the forthcoming release of the final IP Guidelines on distinguishing legitimate exercise of IP and abuse of IP under the AML. Clear definitions and consistent application of the IP Guidelines is essential to give market participants more legal certainty and predictability.

E. Main Themes Covered in This Thesis

This thesis consists of six parts. Following this introduction the author will provide - in the second part – an overview of the Anti-Monopoly Law (AML) of the People's Republic of China (PRC) and its enforcement mechanisms. This part will also elaborate on certain constraints regarding effective enforcement of the law considering current socio-economic development. A comparative study of the Chinese anti-monopoly law and the European competition regime will follow in Part III. Part IV will cover the latest IP Guidelines (2017) under the auspice of the Anti-Monopoly Commission operating under the State Council. These are the very first comprehensive Guidelines that apply competition law to IPRs. Part V will review one of the most important landmark decisions (*Huawei v. InterDigital*) taken by the Chinese courts regarding interaction between competition law and IPR.

On the basis of her analysis, the author will come to the conclusion that each competition system evolves based on its own socio-economic context while at the same time providing a fresh look for other countries which may also at times need to improve their competition policies and judicial regimes.

II. China's Anti-Monopoly Law – A Reflection of the Successful Transition from a Centrally-Planned to a Market Economy

A. Important Milestones

China introduced economic reforms at the end of the 1970s. The ambitious market-oriented measures aimed at encouraging private business, foreign investment through joint ventures (JV) with Chinese enterprises and foreign trade. As a result, competition increased, private sector exploded, and living standards improved. After ten years of fast growth, the annual inflation rate in China skyrocketed to almost 20 percent by the end of the 1980s.[20] In order to control the situation, various austerity measures including tighter monetary controls and limitations of foreign JV projects were adopted in 1988. This "cooling-off" period[21] came to an end following Deng Xiaoping's famous tour to southern China in 1992. Thereafter China was put on a path of renewed and unprecedented economic growth. During this period China accelerated its pace of economic reforms by privatizing and replacing management in state-owned enterprises (SOEs). The "wild capitalism" of the 1990s called for tougher regulations to harness the market disorder. It became imperative to introduce new legal norms to safeguard and enhance competition. The consistent competition policy needs to protect the competitive processes by addressing private sector restraints, and state-initiated arbitrary behaviour.

In 1994 China's 8th National People's Congress (NPC) adopted legislation to have a new Anti-Monopoly Law drafted by the State Economic & Trade Commission (SETC, predecessor of MOFCOM) and the State Administration of Industry & Commerce (SAIC). In the following thirteen years, the drafting group had countless hearings with Chinese and foreign legal and economic experts. Hot debates took place between various Chinese authorities during the drafting process. After three revisions of the

---

20 National Bureau of Statistics of China, available at http://data.stats.gov.cn/search.htm?s=1988 年中国通货膨胀率.

21 Another important factor that led to an economic downturn at that time was related to the Tiananmen Square incident in 1989, which led to subsequent sanctions by Western countries.

draft law, the Chinese Anti-monopoly Law (AML) was finally promulgated and came into effect in 2008. Never before in Chinese legislative history had a drafting and consultation process taken that long before the law came into effect. This illustrates how difficult it is for the Chinese government to balance domestic industrial policies with the conflicting goals of the AML. In addition, enforcing widespread administrative controls under the AML could pose further challenges to governmental authorities and the judiciary alike.[22] Nonetheless, the first modern Chinese competition law has been viewed as a "milestone of the country's efforts in promoting a fair competition market and cracking down on monopoly activities".[23]

B. China's Competition Regime Prior to the AML

Competition policy is not entirely new in China. The starting point for a Chinese competition regime can be traced back to October 1980 when the State Council promulgated an interim *Regulation on Promotion and Protection of Socialist Competition*. Even though the regulation was not effectively enforced, this was a breakthrough in the economic reform process in terms of competition policy.[24] In the following years, legislative bodies have been experimenting with reform measures and have enacted various laws and regulations which are vital to the economic development of China. A brief overview will be provided of the most pertinent laws which contain competition-related stipulations prior to the AML.

1. The Anti-Unfair Competition Law of 1993

The Anti-Unfair Competition Law (AUCL), promulgated in 1993 appears to be rather broad and primarily covers the protection of consumers. Yet, the statute has been a valuable tool in fighting against unfair business practices, including actions against passing-off and trade secret theft. Some provisions contained in the law forbid certain conducts such as tie-

---

22 *Supra* note 3, page 8.
23 Nie Peng, *China's First Anti-monopoly Law Takes Effect,* Xinhua News Agency, August 1, 2008.
24 Carl J. Green and Douglas E. Rosenthal, *Competition Regulation in the Pacific Rim* (Oceana Publications, Inc. 1996) 130.

in sales, price fixing and bid rigging (e.g. Art. 6 and Art. 7 and Art. 11 Art. 15), which are normally part of antitrust law in other jurisdictions.[25] Prior to the AML some companies did infer the AUCL and initiate administrative and private actions against abusive conduct of competitors.

One of the most famous cases under the AUCL was the lawsuit brought by the Chinese battery company *Tsum* against the Japan's *Sony Corporation* for illegal bundling of its InfoLITHIUM batteries in Shanghai in November 2004. The plaintiff claimed that *Sony* abused its dominant market position in China and misused its encryption technology to exclude competitors pursuant to Art. 2 of the AUCL. The encryption by *Sony* foreclosed the market and directly damaged the interests of consumers and competitors alike. *Sony* eliminated fair competition by abusing its market dominance and by creating technical barriers to force consumers to purchase only *Sony* batteries. This way, *Sony* earned monopolist profits by tying products when marketing its camcorders and cameras.[26]

This case involving IPR and bundling sales was regarded as the first IP and anti-competitive court matter in China. However, the court eventually dismissed the plaintiff's claim, ruling that there were no tie-ins. The *Sony* case demonstrated the importance of having a comprehensive anti-monopoly law in China.

The Anti-Unfair Competition Law had been in force for more than twenty years since its first release. In the meantime, the Chinese economic, social and legal environment has changed greatly. New types of unfair competition behaviour have emerged with Internet and online software, which were not listed under the AUCL. Due to the promulgation of the AML, the amended *Trademark Law of PRC* and the amended *Advertising Law of PRC*, there were certain overlappings, ununiformed definitions of terms that need to be deleted or revised. Other stipulations need to

---

25 Bruce M. Owen, Su Sun & Wentong Zheng, *China's Competition Policy Reforms: The Anti-Monopoly Law and Beyond*, 75 Antitrust L.J. 231 (2008), available at http://scholarship.law.ufl.edu/facultypub/223.

26 The Sony InfoLITHIUM batteries Model NP-FP90 was being sold at RMB 890, while the same type of battery from Tsum costed RMB 283. In one year Sony generated a profit of RMB 330 million by selling 550 000 digital devices. Considering that InfoLITHIUM batteries need to be replaced every 1 – 2 years, Sony's additional profit due to tie-ins were significant. See Wang Xianlin, "*Preliminary observations and thoughts on China's first lawsuit concerning anti-monopoly law*", East Law Study (关于中国反垄断诉讼第一案的初步观察与思考, 东方法学), 2006, Issue 2.

be updated and added in order to cover unfair behaviour by using online technology.

On February 26, 2017 the 12ᵗʰ Standing Committee of the NPC released the amendments[27] to the AUCL for public opinion solicitation. In November 2017 the amendments were approved by the Standing Committee of the NPC and the new AUCL became effective on January 1, 2018. What is worth mentioning is that the revised law has significantly increased the range of penalties against violators, from RMB 100 000 to RMB 3 million (about USD 15 000 to USD 460 000).

2. The Price Law of 1997

The Price Law of the PRC was promulgated on December 29, 1997, and became effective on May 1, 1998. This law gives importance to the role of prices for rational allocation of resources. Art. 1 of the law sets the aim of protecting the interests of consumers and business operators by standardizing price behaviour.

The pertinent stipulation on competition policy in this law is Art. 14, which forbids collusive practice to control market price to the detriment of other market participants and consumers. Art. 14(5) explicitly prohibits price discrimination. Art. 40 of the Price Law stipulates that violators of any acts listed in Art. 14 *"shall be ordered to correct, have their illegal proceeds confiscated and be fined concurrently for an amount less than five times the illegal proceeds. In cases of no illegal proceeds involved, a warning shall be issued, together with a fine. For serious cases, they shall be ordered to stop operation for correction or have their business licenses revoked."*

The Price Law has been an important instrument for Chinese authorities to maintain price discipline in economy, especially when prices relate to consumer products and services. One of the landmark decisions under the Price Law was the administrative sanction issued by the NDRC against the company *Unilever* for "disseminating information to the public anticipat-

---

27 Out of the current thirty-three articles of AUCL, amendments were made to thirty provisions: seven articles were deleted, nine articles were added. The revised version composes of thirty-five article in total. Available at http://www.legaldaily.com.cn/Finance_and_Economics/content/2017-04/05/content_7080645.htm?node=76109.

ing price increases, thus distorting the market price order".[28] The NDRC and the Shanghai Price Administration Bureau found that *Unilever* deliberately spread such information at various press interviews, which gave time to Unilever's competitors to align their prices for similar products accordingly. Factually, competitors responded by taking similar actions, and this caused panic purchasing in various Chinese cities in 2011. The NDRC further specified in the statement that this prior signaling helped to achieve a *price cartel* without significant changes in market shares among existing competitors in the industry. *Unilever* was compelled to rectify its violations and had to pay a fine of RMB two million (around USD 300,000).[29] This was the first highly publicized price-related law enforcement action against a multinational company in China.

C. The Anti-Monopoly Law Comes into Force

When considering the AUCL and the Price Law, one may conclude that the Chinese competition regime prior to the enactment of the AML was fragmented. Isolated laws and administrative rules tried to deal with competition issues as they arose along with the economic reform and modernizations process in China.[30] Different authorities were mandated by different laws to enforce anticompetitive behaviour.[31] In contrast, all AML stipulations promote fair competition and combat monopoly activities. The AML prohibits monopolistic conduct in the following areas:

– Monopoly agreements between business operators (Chapter II)
– Abuse of dominant market position by business operators (Chapter III)
– Concentration of business operators which may have the effect of eliminating competition (Chapter IV), and
– Abuse of administrative powers for elimination of competition (Chapter V)

---

28 News released on the official website of NDRC, *Unilever, "High Penalty"*(联合利华，高额处罚") available at http://xwzx.ndrc.gov.cn/mtfy/zymt/201105/t20110512_411787.html.
29 *NDRC: Unilever Was Fined RMB Two Millions for Spreading Rumors of Price Rising* (发改委: 联合利华散布涨价信息被罚 200 万), available at http://finance.qq.com/a/20110506/002832.htm.
30 *Supra* note 25.
31 *Id.*

Apart from Chapter V, which addresses administrative monopoly in the country[32], the AML adopted the "three pillar" system of modern competition law. It comprises eight chapters and 57 articles, which cover the following areas:

	Main Topics of Each Chapter	Article numbers
Chapter 1	General principles of AML: Objectives, applicability, coverage, role of SOEs in important sectors, role of trade associations	Articles 1 – 12
Chapter 2	Classification of types of prohibited monopoly agreements	Articles 13 – 16
Chapter 3	Prohibition of abuse of market dominant position; criteria of judging market dominance; description of abusive conduct	Articles 17 – 19
Chapter 4	Concentration of business operators: mergers & acquisition, JVs.	Articles 20 – 31
Chapter 5	Prohibition of anticompetitive activities by government agencies, particularly forbidding various forms of local protectionism	Articles 32 – 37
Chapter 6	Description of investigative procedures to be followed by enforcement agencies	Articles 38 – 45
Chapter 7	Liability and penalties for violating the AML	Articles 46 – 54
Chapter 8	Supplementary provisions IPR is not per se unlawful monopoly, but abuse of such rights is subject to the AML	Articles 55 – 57

---

32 Due to the long history of planned economy there are still regional and industrial monopolies. For instance, local governments may refuse to issue business licenses to business operators coming from another province. Ministries and their subsidiaries from certain key industry sectors (e.g. petroleum) use their administrative powers to designate only specific companies to operate in that sector.

Art. 55 is the only IP related provision. It is worth noticing that Art. 55 of the AML, though very general, established the relationship between IPR and the anti-competition regime, which reads as follows:

"This Law shall not apply to the exercise of intellectual property by business operators pursuant to the relevant laws and administrative regulations on intellectual property; however, this Law shall apply to the abuse of intellectual property by business operators to exclude or restrict competition."

This provision offers IPR holders a safe harbour but also explicitly prevents the abuse of IPR rights.[33] The basic principle of the interplay between the IPR regime and Chinese competition policy is thus highlighted. However, no definition or framework is provided on the boundaries between legitimate practice of IP rights and abuse of exclusive rights. The recently published IP Guidelines attempt to provide more clarity on these issues, which will be discussed in greater detail in Chapter IV.

D. Institutional Design of Competition Agencies under the AML

1. Administrative enforcement agencies

According to Articles 9 and 10 of the AML, two levels of regulatory agencies are established:
- Anti-Monopoly Commission (AMC) under the State Council: responsible for studying and drafting relevant competition policy, organising market investigation, formulating guidelines and coordinating competition administrative enforcement tasks.
- Anti-Monopoly Enforcement Authority (AMEA) designated by the State Council, which is responsible for the enforcement of the AML

The AMC does not enforce the law directly, but rather supervises and coordinates AML-related activities. A group of legal and economic experts provides advice to the Commission for tackling major issues in the field of competition.

It is no secret that heavy debates on institutional design of competition enforcement agencies behind the scenes also largely contributed to the de-

---

33 Dr. Yijun Tian, *The Impacts of the Chinese Anti-Monopoly Law on IP Commercialization in China & General Strategies for Technology-Driven Companies and Future Regulators*, Duke Law & Technology Review, 2010.

lay of the adoption of AML. Finally, three government agencies acting under the Chinese State Council, and enjoying ministry status, were empowered to rule over competition enforcement in China. Depending on the abusive conduct, responsibilities are allocated as follows:

– The National Development and Reform Commission (NDRC): Enforcing price related rules of the AML, including anti-competitive agreements and abuse of dominant position

– The State Administration of Industry and Commerce (SAIC): Enforcing non-price related rules of the AML, including abuse of administrative powers

– The Ministry of Commerce (MOFCOM): Enforcing merger controls.

Some scholars and practitioners expressed their concerns on possible lack of efficiency and consistency regarding decision makings derived from the tripartite system.[34] Others argued that decentralization of enforcement and competition among agencies might improve the quality of work.[35] Some referred to the US which has a dual enforcement system consisting of the Antitrust Division of the Department of Justice (DOJ) and the Federal Trade Commission (FTC) sharing responsibility of enforcing federal antitrust law. A single competition enforcement agency may not be necessarily the best option, as evidenced by Japan's Fair Trade Commission (JFTC).[36] The Chinese tripartite enforcement system can advantageously tap the experiences and strength that each agency had early obtained in its own field prior to the adoption of the AML.

Friction can indeed exist and investigation tasks might overlap between SAIC and NDRC. Supposing that monopolists and oligopolists are engaged in both price-related and non-price related anticompetitive conducts such as charging excessive patent royalty fees, abusing dominant positions, or having restrictive agreements, both authorities could practically become involved. In order to avoid conflict, NDRC and SAIC adopted implementation rules[37] for enforcement of the AML and divided their responsibilities in 2011.

---

34 Xiaoye Wang, *Highlights of China's New Anti-Monopoly Law*, 75 Antitrust L.J 133, 144-46, 2008.

35 *Supra* note 3, page 130.

36 *Supra* note 3, page 130.

37 NDRC : *Anti-Pricing Monopoly Rules* promulgated by on 29 December, 2010 (反 价 格 垄 断 规 定), available at http://www.gov.cn/flfg/2011-01/04/ content_1777969.htm; SAIC: *Rules on the Prohibition of Abusing Dominant Mar-*

Responsibilities of NDRC and SAIC

	NDRC	**SAIC**
Restrictive agreement	Price fixing	Restriction of output/sales; division of sales, division of raw material markets; boycotting
Abuse of dominant position	Resale price maintenance, predatory pricing, unfairly high or low prices	Refusal to deal, exclusive dealing, bundling, tying and discriminatory treatment

2. Judicial enforcement

Numerous Chinese companies and individuals could barely wait to take judicial actions based on the AML. On August 1, 2008 when the AML became effective, three cases were brought to courts. At initial stages it was very difficult for plaintiffs to collect evidence for lack of information and sufficient economic knowledge by Chinese courts to determine violations. Till the end of 2011 totally 61 cases were filed at first instance nationwide, of which 53 were concluded by settlement or final ruling.[38] Hundreds of other cases were dismissed by courts, and where final court ruling was taken, it was mainly defendants who prevailed. The situation started changing after the Supreme People's Court (SPC) issued the "Monopoly Case Provision"[39] taking into account past judicial experiences in China and abroad and addressing essential issues such as jurisdiction, plaintiff qualification and allocation of burden of proof.

In the following years, the number of civil enforcement cases increased drastically and even exceeded those filed with public enforcement agen-

---

ket Positions (工商行政管理机关禁止垄断协议行为的规定), available at http:// www.gov.cn/flfg/2011-01/07/content_1779945.htm.

38 SPC Issued the First Judicial Interpretations on the AML, Private Parties Can Sue Monopolistic Enterprises Directly (最高人民法院出台反垄断审判第一部司法解释公民可直接起诉垄断企业), May 9, 2012, available at http://www.66law.cn/ topic2010/fldspsfjs/21162.shtml.

39 On May 3, 2012 the Supreme People's Court published "*Provision on the Application of Laws in Civil Disputes Cases Arising from Monopoly Activities*", Chinese version available at http://legal.people.com.cn/GB/17836437.html.

cies (AMEAs).[40]Judicial enforcement has made considerable progress. According to the IP Tribunal of the SPC, there is room for further improvement including optimization in the allocation of burden of proof, evidence deposition by courts, expert witness and opinion at courts. It is also vital for judges to better assess economic and market report, and improve their financial skills. Overreliance on market share threshold could lead to biased decisions especially in new economy sectors.[41]

E. Future Challenges

It is highly debatable whether emerging economies like China should open their markets to competition without limitations, or whether they also need to protect their own national industries and start-up enterprises for the sake of broad public interest. One of the focal issues will be to strike a balance between a modern competition law and indispensable industrial and innovation policies aimed at serving the long-term interest of the country. Another area of concern are China's state-owned enterprises (SOEs) which still dominate certain industries such as finance, defense, raw materials, energy, transportation and infrastructure as well as local administrative powers which may hinder the effective enforcement of competition law.

Art. 7 of the AML explicitly forbids large-scale SOEs from using their controlling or exclusive dealing position to harm the interests of consumers. Art. 7 also calls for public supervision of the behaviour of those companies. It is still questionable that competition agencies remain neutral in assessing abusive conduct from such companies given that their management and shareholdings are controlled by the State-owned Assets Supervision and Administration Commission of the State Council (SASAC), which is also a state body. On the other hand, the Chinese government will have to continue playing an essential role in improving economic efficiency by using SOEs as a vehicle while optimizing their operations. It should

---

40 Wang Chuang, IP Tribunal of Supreme People's Court,"*Overview and Perspective of Civil Enforcement under the AML*" (中国反垄断民事诉讼概况及展望), "... From commencement of the AML in August 2008 till December 2015, 430 civil suits have been filed with Chinese courts in comparison with less than 100 cases filed with the competition agencies.", Competition Policy Research, March Issue, 2016, available at http://www.doc88.com/p-3959736501814.html.

41 *Id.*

be in the interest of a country to privatise state assets in a supervised way. Lessons from the aftermath of the collapse of the Soviet Union which pursued an approach of uncontrolled massive privitisations could be drawn by other transitional economies.

Articles 32 to 37 of the AML prohibit the abuse of power by administrative, regional and sectoral monopolies. However, in the case of abuse the AMEAs are not empowered to impose any sanctions, but only to submit opinions to the corresponding "superior authorities" and to ask them to correct the anticompetitive conduct. The greatest challenge here is the possible lack of neutrality and transparency in enforcing decisions because of the long legacy of entrenched local interests.

Art. 33 of the AML specifically addresses the issue of regional protectionism, forbidding local and regional authorities to abuse their powers to restrict free circulation of commodities between different provinces of China and prevent companies from other regions to establish more effective operations. The Chinese government is aware of the detrimental effect that regional protectionism may have on the national economy because of losses of allocative resources.

In the future, China will definitely make efforts to converge its competition regime with international standards. The adoption of the AML is a clear achievement of a county moving forward on its path toward a true market economy. In turn, China's economic reforms will be further accelerated by the successful adoption and enforcement of its competition law.

III. EU Competition Policy – Main Reference for China's Anti-Monopoly Law

A. Background Information

In 1980, only fifteen countries worldwide had a competition law. Today this number arose to nearly 130. For almost a century the United States had been the unmistakable center for global competition policy since the passage of the Sherman Act in 1890.[42] With the establishment and expansion of the European common market, by the twenty first century, the EU competition law has extended its influence further to other parts of the world and obtained increasing recognition by younger jurisdictions such as China. The transitional process from monopoly to duopoly and to oligopoly has already begun.[43]

Many countries in the world have now introduced their versions of competition laws. With falling trade barriers and tariffs worldwide, particularly under the framework of WTO, increasing number of companies operate on a global scale. They are constantly exposed to legal systems and business practices that exist in different countries. They will appreciate efforts by authorities to harmonise competition law norms. Whereas the US and the EU are founding members of the *informal* International Competition Network (ICN) covering about 120 jurisdictions, China has not yet joined the network.

Given China's growing influence in the world, both the EU and the US experts had been trying to advocate their competition law norms. Finally, the EU competition law became the major reference of China's Anti-Monopoly Law (AML). Yet, the AML is not simply a blueprint of the EU competition law, but also includes its own country specific elements.

---

42 William E. Kovacic, *The United States and Its Future Influence on Global Competition Policy,* George Mason Law Review, 2015, 1157 – 1204, available at http://www.georgemasonlawreview.org/wp-content/uploads/22_5_Kovacic.pdf.

43 William E. Kovacic, Dominance, Duopoly and Oligopoly: *The United States and the Development of Global Competition Policy,* Global Competition Review, December 2010.

B. Why the US Competition Law Did Not Serve As the Main Model?

There are numerous reasons which prevented China from taking the US system as reference. The statutory language of the US antitrust law ("Sherman Act") is rather general; it just lays down major principles such as "restraint of free trade" and "monopolization". In the absence of competition institutions or guidance, US judges need to interpret the statutes and articulate the goals of competition law.[44] China is basically a civil law country, and there is no tradition of relying on court rulings for interpreting the law.

In addition, under the influence of the "law-and-economics" approach the US courts interpret goals of antitrust law in a very narrow sense, purely based on criteria of market efficiency.[45] US antitrust policy puts strong belief in self-correction of the market and less intervention. By seeking a single economic objective, other values such as environmental protections, non-discrimination and fairness are often neglected. Competition should be the means to achieve the ultimate goal, i.e. "improvement of well-being", rather than as an aim *per se*.[46] For a transitional economy like China, where market conditions and mechanisms were not yet available as in the US, it would have been too risky to leave everything to the market. The market failure with sometimes disastrous economic consequences for developing countries which mechanically followed the *Washington Consensus* is another proof of great danger in case of simple-mindedly implementation of US ideology without considering the specific socio-economic environment in the country.[47] Arguably, the assumption of "self-correcting"

---

44 David J. Gerber, *Constructing Competition Law in China: The Potential Value of European and U.S. Experience,* Washington University Global Studies Law Review, January 2004.

45 *Id.*

46 Stucke, Maurice E., Reconsidering Antitrust's Goals (August 3, 2011). Boston College Law Review, Vol. 53, p. 551, 2012; University of Tennessee Legal Studies Research Paper No. 163. Available at SSRN: https://ssrn.com/abstract=1904686.

47 Washington Consensus refers to a set of free market economic ideas, supported by prominent economists from the US and the EU, and international organisations such as World Bank, International Monetary Fund (IMF) and the US Treasury. The core concept of the consensus is for free markets, free trade and floating exchange rates. From the ten specific policy reforms advocated, one might conclude that the driving forces behind the principles are the interests from large multinationals and financial institutions. It is widely believed that mechanical transplanting the principles led to the macro-economic crisis in Latin America in the 1980s and the seri-

is also composed of rational, self-interested market participants[48] which could create significant political pressure on policy-makers.

Apart from the sole aim of US antitrust law, US courts are the main implementers and enforcers of the law. The US experience is no valuable reference for China, whose administrative powers are strong at both central and local levels. Also China's current socio-economic environment does not allow it to focus only on market efficiency.

In comparison with the US, the EU competition regime has been relying more on legislative processes. The market integration of EU Member States by using competition policy as a vehicle can bring valuable experience to overcome China's artificial regional restrictions of trade and business. In addition, ten new European countries joined the EU in 2004, most of them being former communist countries.[49] Privatizing, reforming and integrating these countries' state-owned companies into a market system under the EU competition rules could provide valuable expertise for China.

The US and EU competition regimes differ greatly as they are embedded in different political, economic and cultural environments, and resulting in different enforcement agencies. In the following, a few aspects of similarities and differences between the EU and Chinese competition law systems are analysed in more detail.

C. Comparison Between EU and Chinese Competition Regimes

1. Multiple goals

The EU competition policy was significantly influenced by German competition law. The early form of German competition law, the *Kartellverordnung,* played an important role in German economic and legal

---

ous economic crisis in South East Asia in the 1990s. See also Tejvan Pettinger, *Criticism of IMF*, November 28, 2012, available at http://www.economicshelp.org/blog/glossary/imf-criticism/ and *Washington Consensus – Definition and Criticism*, April 25, 2013, available at
http://www.economicshelp.org/blog/7387/economics/washington-consensus-definition-and-criticism/.

48 *Supra* note 46.

49 Cyprus, the Czech Republic, Estonia, Hungary, Latvia, Lithuania, Malta, Poland, Slovakia, and Slovenia.

regimes during the Weimar Republic.[50] The primary aim of the German legislation was to put powerful corporations under control so that the competition process including small business and consumers should not be harmed.[51] The German history after the World War II also demonstrated that the state government strongly promoted a "social market economy". The German ideology of giving everybody equal chances to develop is engraved in the society. Doubtlessly, a nation's history, political and economic forces may subsequently predetermine certain features of its competition law system.[52] The German Unfair Competition Law (*Gesetz gegen den Unlauteren Wettbewerb - UWG*) is another good example to protect consumers as well as to promote fair competition. Small and medium-sized companies should have a fair chance to participate in economic activities. No wonder, the single concern of market efficiency of the US antitrust law cannot be attributed to German competition law. Similar to Germany, social democratic politicians in numerous other European countries also attach great value to equal opportunity, and to consumer and employee protection.

Against this European socio-economic and political background, and in view of multi-level governance and the desire of economic integration of the Member States, the European Commission and Courts have devised a specific European Community competition policy with multiple objectives. Apart from efficiency consideration, i.e. enhancing consumer welfare by stimulating both allocative and productive efficiency, the European competition policy protects freedom of individual rights and economic freedom of market competitors as well as broader public interests.[53] According to the EU Commission Annual Report on Competition Policy 2010, multiple objectives of competition regime were explicitly recognized: "... *two clearly identifiable threads run through the entire history of EU competition policy: its contribution to the construction and preservation of the internal market and its contribution to consumer welfare. At the same time, competition policy has supported the main objectives of the Union as set out in the Treaties: a competitive market, economic, social*

---

50 David J. Gerber, *Law and Competition in Twentieth Century Europe: Protecting Prometheus*, (Oxford University Press, 1998) 69 – 114.

51 *Supra* note 44.

52 *Supra* note 42.

53 Wolf Sauter, *Competition Law and Industrial Policy in the EU (*Oxford University Press, 1997) 116-117.

and territorial cohesion and sustainable development"[54] The establishment and expansion of the European Union is a constant process of integrating new member states and balancing a variety of interests among different countries.

Like the EU competition law system, the Chinese AML also confers multiple objectives to its competition regime. Art. 1 of AML lists a series of objectives: protecting fair market competition, promoting efficiency, safeguarding consumer interests and the public interest, and "promoting steady development of the socialist market economy". In comparison with the objectives of the EU competition policy, the core language of the AML such as protection of competition and efficiency, safeguarding interests of consumers and the society, promotion of development bears strong resemblance to EU practice.

It is useful for young jurisdictions to learn from the experience and know-how of more mature jurisdictions, which have already gone through a "trial and error" process.[55] Even borrowing the language of the legislation is important, because certain terms have been proved to be effective and are accorded specific meanings. This tends to give more predictability and legal certainty.[56]

Statute language is one aspect, and effective enforcement of legislation is another. Statutes and implementing institutions is one of the three basic elements for a competition law system.[57] Enforcing the law and regulations in a consequent and consistent manner is essential for market participants. This involves well-trained administrators and experienced judges, but for a young jurisdiction this is not an easy task, let alone other structural and economic impediments entrenched in a society like China.

---

54 European Commission, *Report on Competition Policy 2010*, available at http://ec.europa.eu/competition/publications/annual_report/2010/part1_en.pdf.

55 *Supra* note 44.

56 *Supra* note 44.

57 *Supra* note 42. Competition law systems have three basic elements: statues and implementing institutions, applied analytical methods and procedures, and know-how accumulated during the course of implementing the statute framework and relevant rules.

2. Institutional design and enforcement

2.1. Significance of administrative route for both jurisdictions

At their early stages, competition law systems in many European countries were just a marginal element within the framework of general economic policy. These systems were embedded in economic regulatory frameworks, which were rarely supported by significant political, economic or intellectual forces.[58] It is noteworthy that German *Ordoliberalism* has far-reaching impact on the competition policy in the European common market. This concept assumes that the objective of competition policy should be to protect the independence of the activities of companies and that economic efficiency is a derivative of this aim.[59] *Ordoliberalism* emphasizes the need for the state to create proper legal environment for the economy and maintain a healthy level of competition. Consequently, the starting point for competition law development in Europe involved economic controls supervised by a group of administrators.[60] These administrators with high social status and usually political power would naturally make competition rules that rely on administrative enforcement.[61]

Ordoliberalism became not only the basis for the new German competition law in 1957[62], but also a useful tool for the European Community to eliminate obstacles for trade across national borders.[63] To this end, the European Commission is the body who has the responsibility to develop rules and principles, and to ensure the effective applications of the EU competition policy. Decisions of the Commission are subject to judicial review by the European Court of Justice and the Court of First Instance.

The above points, particularly advocacy for state interference, have extensive reference value for Chinese decision-makers. In view of the fact that the Chinese government and local bureaucracies have strong power to control Chinese economic development and reform process, institutional

---

58 *Supra* note 44.
59 W Möschel, "Competition Policy from an Ordo Point of View", A Peacock and H Willgerodt (eds), *German Neo-Liberals and the Social Market Economy* (Macmillan, 1989).
60 *Supra* note 44.
61 *Supra* note 44.
62 The German competition law *Gesetz gegen Wettbewerbsbeschränkungen* became effective on January 1, 1958. The latest amended version was made in 1998.
63 *Supra* note 44.

design for enforcement would consequently rely on administrative organs rather than on judicial decisions. Chinese policy-makers were able to draw on the experience and knowhow from the European competition policy for privatization and elimination of trade barriers by using competition policy as an effective vehicle. As discussed in Part II, the enacted AML adopted a tripartite enforcement system based on each agency's traditional jurisdictional competence.[64]

2.2. Growing importance of private actions in both jurisdictions

Apart from public administrative enforcement, private court actions are a complementary mechanism to ensure effective enforcement of competition law. In comparison with the US competition regime, the EU Commission acknowledges certain weaknesses in the enforcement system due to shortage of private actions. Giving victims of anticompetitive conduct the possibility to claim compensation for losses is probably one of the most effective ways to deter anticompetitive conducts. The staggering figure of Euro 3.7 billion fines imposed by the European Commission in 2016[65] on violators of competition rules sets a sign for further strengthening of the competition enforcement. To this end, the European Union issued the new *Directive on certain rules governing actions for damages under national law for infringements of the competition law provisions of the Member States and of the European Union* (Damages Directive).[66] The *Damages Directive* makes it much easier for victims of anticompetitive violations to claim compensations. It is poised to fine-tune the interplay between private damages claims and public enforcement.[67]

Likewise in China, it is possible to bring anti-monopoly lawsuits to a competent court pursuant to Art. 50 of the AML, and Articles 1 and 2 of the *Supreme People's Court Provisions on Monopolistic Conduct*. Private actions in China were further encouraged after the issuance of the

---

64 See Part II, D1.
65 Cartel Statistics, available at http://ec.europa.eu/competition/cartels/statistics/statistics.pdf.
66 DIRECTIVE 2014/104/EU OF THE EUROPEAN PARLIAMENT AND OF THE COUNCIL of 26 November 2014.
67 European Commission, Competition Policy Brief, The Damages Directive, January 2015, available at European Commission, Competition Policy Brief, January 2015.

Monopoly Case Provision by the Supreme People's Court (SPC) in 2012.[68] The burden of proof to be brought by the victims of anticompetitive conduct has been alleviated considerably in recent years in China. For instance, in the case of horizontal agreements defendants bear the burden of proof. But for vertical agreements, the burden of proof lies with the plaintiff, unless under special circumstances courts may order defendants to provide evidence.[69] Stipulations in the EU *Damages Directives* also give victims easier access to evidence needed to prove the suffered damages.

Similar to the EU, administrative decisions from the competition authorities in China are subject to judicial review, and a follow-on civil action can be filed at a competent court.Neither the EU nor Chinese competition regime includes criminal liability for violation of competition laws, and both systems rely on fines.

3. Legal framework and comparison of stipulations

The legal structure of the enacted Chinese AML is comparable to that of the EU, in which three areas are regulated: anticompetitive agreements, abuse of market dominance and mergers. In the EU competition regime, the general principles of these three mentioned areas are laid down in Articles 101 and 102 in the *Treaty on the Functioning of the European Union* (TFEU). Detailed guidance on implementation of these principles is given in numerous Council Regulations of the EU. One example is the Commission Regulation on Technology Transfer Agreements[70] which gives guidance on implementing Art. 101(3) TFEU.

Like in the EU and many other jurisdictions, the Chinese AML is also rather general.[71] In order to apply the AML consistently, all three Chinese competition agencies and the Supreme People's Court have released vari-

---

68 *Supra* note 39.
69 *Supra* note 39.
70 Commission Regulation (EU), 316/2014 on the application of Article 101(3) of the Treaty on the Functioning of the European Union to categories of technology transfer agreements.
71 For instance, Art. 1 sets multiple goals for Chinese competition policy. One of them is public interest. Yet, no definition on public interest is made. Art. 2 sets forth "extraterritoriality" principle, but it is very too broad. "...*this Law shall apply to monopoly acts outside the People's Republic of China which eliminate or*

ous provisions and regulations for implementing the AML in their specific jurisdictions. For instance, the *State Council Guideline on Definition of Relevant Market*[72], released on July 7, 2009 follows closely the *Commission Notice on Definition of Relevant Market* (EC Notice) released in 1997.[73] The Chinese guidelines include well-established EU principles, although they are less detailed and certain aspects are not covered.[74] Conclusively, the Chinese legal hierarchy between primary law (AML) and the secondary legislation (implementing rules and regulations) is similar to the EU competition regime.

Articles 13 and 14 of the AML govern horizontal and vertical monopolistic agreements respectively. The combined content of these two stipulations is derived from Article 101 (1) TFEU. But their enumerations are non-exhaustive. Owing to the tradition, in China more discretionary power is conferred to the administrative authorities. Interestingly, the enumerations in Articles 101 (1) and 102 TFEU are also open-ended.[75]

Art. 15 of the AML resembles 101(3) TFEU closely, but it provides much broader exemptions than the exemption rules under 101(3) TFEU.

The EU competition policy clearly acknowledges that some restrictive agreements may generate economic benefits which outweigh negative effects of the restriction of competition. Pursuant to the guidelines on the application of Art. 101(3) TFEU, an agreement must satisfy four cumulative conditions as follows:

– It must contribute to improving the production or distribution of goods or contribute to promoting technical or economic progress,
– Consumers must receive a fair share of the resulting benefits

---

restrict market competition in China". Art. 55 concerns the interface between competition law and IPR which is just a very general statement (cf. Page 19).

72 Chinese   version   available   at   http://www.gov.cn/zwhd/2009-07/07/content_1355288.htm.

73 Official Journal of the European Communities, 97/C 372/03, available at http://eur-lex.europa.eu/legal-content/EN/TXT/PDF/?uri=CELEX:31997Y1209(01)&from=EN.

74 For example, in the EC Notice it is recognized that in the case of primary and secondary markets and chains of substitution, the usual principles need to be applied cautiously. EC Notice acknowledges that a definitive conclusion on market definition may not be required in every case, while Chinese regulations are silent on that. See also Yvonne Percival et al, *Comments on China's Guidelines on Market Definition*, available at https://www.lexology.com/library/detail.aspx?g=8013ec2d-b9b7-4acc-b109-199ab0236816.

75 *Tetra Pak International v. Commission*, C-333/94 P, [1996] ECR I-05951 [37].

– The restrictions must be indispensable to the attainment of these objectives, and
– The agreement must not afford the parties the possibility of eliminating competition in respect of a substantial part of the products in question.[76]

The conditions laid down in Art. 101(3) must be met *cumulatively*, otherwise no exemption will apply. In contrast thereto, Art. 15 of the AML provides that monopolistic agreements caught under Articles 13 and 14 of the AML may be exempted based on *one of the five following grounds*: (1) technological improvement (2) improvement of product quality and efficiency (3) market inclusiveness of small and medium-sized companies (4) public interest such as energy conservation, environmental protection, disaster relief, etc. (5) mitigating severe decrease in sales volume during economic recessions. Factors (6) and (7) in the list provide protection of legitimate interests in foreign trade, and any other circumstances stipulated by the State Council respectively. The first three conditions are modelled after Art. 101(3) TFEU, although the wording adopted by the AML is slightly different.

Pursuant to Art. 15 AML, each of the aforementioned five conducts is procompetitive, which will set off the negative anticompetitive effect of a monopolistic agreement. Art. 15 (4) concerns public interest, and the list of factors given therein is not exhaustive. There are concerns that such broad exemptions provided in Art. 15 would significantly limit the applicable scope of the AML.[77] Yet, Art. 15 also specifies that business operator must prove that the agreement "*will not severely restrict competition in the relevant market, and will allow consumers to benefit from the interests arising therefrom*". Contents of these two mentioned criteria reflect part of the four conditions set by the Art. 101(3) TFEU. But the indispensability of the restrictions to achieve the objectives is missing here, which subsequently makes the exemption rules less strict. Furthermore, based on Art. 101(3) TFEU, consumers must obtain a "fair share of the resulting benefit", while the AML omits the adjective "fair" without further specifying the degree of participation by consumers.

---

76 *Exempted Agreements (Article 101(3) TFEU)*, available at http://ec.europa.eu/competition/antitrust/legislation/art101_3_en.html.
77 Peter J. Wang et al., New Chinese Anti-Monopoly Law, October 2007, available at http://www.jonesday.com/New_Chinese_Anti-Monopoly_Law/.

Conditions (6) and (7) specified in Art. AML 15 are elements which do not appear in the EU competition law. Arguably, Art. 15 (6) may be interpreted as a stipulation to enable Chinese companies to compete in international trade.

D. *Dynamics of Competition Policy*

The AML appears to be a successful legal transplant from the European competition law into China based on the country's socio-economic environment. Political and economic interests confer competition policy with different priority goals at different stages. This makes competition law a very dynamic regime. A holistic viewpoint is helpful to understand various paradigms of competition policy. From the EU experience it could be argued that competition policy evolves in close relationship with the development of the European common market. Thus, the primary goals of the EU competition law have also been altered in the last decades. Up to the 1990s the main objective of the EU competition policy was to support efforts of market integration. Once that phase was more or less concluded, the Commission and the Courts seem to be more willing to embrace the Chicago and post-Chicago insights, which only focus on economic aspects of market efficiency. Hitherto, there are reasons to believe that the Chinese competition law will in future be more effectively and objectively enforced with the deepening of the country's economic and legal reforms.

IV. China's 2017 IP Guidelines

A. *China at the Crossroads between Competition Enforcement and Intellectual Property Rights*

The interplay between competition law and IPR protection has been increasingly in the focus of competition enforcement authorities in many jurisdictions including China. The landmark judgement on *Huawei v. Inter-Digital* (covered in depth in the next chapter) and the *Qualcomm* decision issued by NDRC demonstrated that both judicial and governmental bodies are willing to deal with complex IPR-related matters.[78] After the landmark decision on *Qualcomm* in 2015 which resulted in an unprecedented fine, the Chinese competition authorities put other IP-intensive sectors under scrutiny. Specific attention is being paid to telecommunication, pharmaceuticals, medical equipment, automotive, agro-machineries and plant varieties.

However, in the absence of clear guidelines on IPR-related monopolistic conduct, IPR owners and investors have concerns as to which practice would constitute violation of Art. 55 of the AML. It is therefore imperative to provide more detailed guidance to specify the boundary between legitimate exercise of IPRs and abuses of the rights to eliminate or restrict competition.

So far all three Chinese enforcement agencies were making efforts to develop guidelines on assessment of IPRs under the AML. Currently the *"Provisions on Prohibition of Abuse of Intellectual Property Rights to Exclude and Restrict Competition" (Provisions)* released by SAIC on April 7, 2015 represented the only legal document serving as a basis for its enforcement against IPR-related anticompetitive conducts. The Provisions aim to balance the lawful interests of IPR owners and other relevant parties, and impose enforcement against AML violators. However, as discussed in Part II, SAIC is merely empowered to enforce non-price related violations. Therefore, its *Provisions* have inherent deficiencies when it

---

78 Slaughter and May, *Competition Law in China*, November 2016, available at https://www.slaughterandmay.com/media/879862/competition-law-in-china.pdf.

comes to violation of the AML regarding price-related or merger control issues.

Despite insufficient coverage, SAIC's endeavor to explore the complex area of interplay between IPR and competition law has provided valuable experience for further development of rules.

B. Characteristics and Main Principles of the IP Guidelines

Under the coordination of the China's Anti-Monopoly Commission (AMC) operating on behalf of the State Council, the first draft of the *Anti-Monopoly Guidelines on the Abuse of Intellectual Property Rights (Draft for Comments)* ("IP Guidelines") was published in Chinese on March 23, 2017.[79] These Guidelines combined issues from the three competition agencies and taking into account the opinion of the State Intellectual Property Office (SIPO).

The *IP Guidelines* are composed of five chapters with a total of 27 articles covering the following issues:

	Issues Covered	
Chapter 1	General issues: analytical principles, framework; relevant market; factors to be considered in assessing anti-competitive effects; conditions for establishing positive effects	Articles 1 – 5
Chapter 2	Restrictive agreements relating to IPRs: joint R&D, cross licensing, exclusive grant-back, non-challenging clause, standard setting, safe harbour criteria	Articles 6 – 12
Chapter 3	Abuse of dominant market position involving IPRs	Articles13 – 18
Chapter 4	Concentration of business operators involving IPRs	Articles 19 – 24
Chapter 5	Other circumstances involving IPRs	Articles 25 – 27

---

79 Chinese version available at http://fldj.mofcom.gov.cn/article/zcfb/201703/20170302539418.shtml.

1. Principles of analysis – Art. 1

Art. 1 of the Guidelines provides four basic principles to be respected when assessing whether exercise of IPRs excludes or restricts competition.
– The first principle sets forth that basic analytical framework needs to be consistent with that of the AML.
– The second principle states consideration of specific characteristics of IPRs.
– The third principle acknowledges that there is no presumption of market dominance simply due to ownership of IPRs.
– The fourth principle calls for consideration of positive effects of efficiency and innovation upon assessment of relevant conducts on a *case by case* basis.
The third principle provides IP owners with legal certainty. However, situation could become controversial depending on how relevant product market is defined. As will be discussed in the *Huawei v. InterDigital* case in Part V, the Chinese courts tend to adopt a very narrow approach in defining the product market for SEP owners; so did NDRC in its decision on *Qualcomm* case.

The fourth principle seems to suggest that the Guidelines took a more cautious approach, i.e. each case is different, and more factors need to be taken into consideration when assessing IP-related conduct under the AML. One may take it as a positive sign that the policy-makers admitted the complexity between granted exclusivity of IPR on the one hand and competition concerns on the other. Arguably, this is a hint that the authorities would value the importance that dynamic efficiency could bring, particularly prospective market effects generated by the new economy.

2. Safe harbour principle – Art. 12

Art. 12 of the Guidelines specifies three criteria on IPR-related agreements, and meeting any of them will not be considered monopoly agreements, as set in Articles 13(6) and 14(3) of the AML
(a) aggregate shares of undertakings in a competitive relationship in the relevant market do not exceed 20 percent
(b) Shares of undertakings in a non-competitive relationship in any relevant market do not exceed 30 percent

(c) In case market shares of relevant undertakings are difficult to obtain, or market shares are unable to reflect the market position of the undertakings, there should exist four or more than four substitutable technologies on the relevant market that are independently controlled by other undertakings and obtainable *at reasonable costs*[80] in addition to the technology controlled by the relevant parties to the agreement.

Art. 12 of the Guidelines aims at providing "efficient enforcement, offering clear prospects for market stakeholders".[81] The purpose of this stipulation is to suggest that any agreement which fulfills the above criteria will not fall into the scope of Art. 13(6) and Art. 14(3) of the AML, and thus will not be considered as monopolistic conduct. The safe harbour principle in the Guidelines provides guidance and better predictability for IPR owners. However, it is undefined what costs would be "reasonable costs" for obtaining alternative technologies in relevant market. Future public enforcement and court rulings need to interpret and set benchmarks.

The requirement of market shares of Art. 12 of the Guidelines for competing and non-competing undertakings is in line with Art. 3 of the EU Commission Regulation on "Technology Transfer Block Exemption Regulation" (TTBER).[82] Unlike in the TTBER, the "hardcore restrictions"[83] were not mentioned in the Chinese Guidelines. In the absence of a clear delineation of the scope of hardcore restrictions on price fixing, output constraints, market and customer allocations, the exemption defined by the "safe harbour principle" might practically have not much effect.[84]

3. Refusal to license IPRs – Art. 15

"Essential facilities doctrine" imposes on owners of essential facility the duty to deal with competitors in order to maintain competition. This doctrine is not mentioned anywhere in the enacted AML. Art. 15 of the

---

80 Emphasis added.

81 Original Chinese text of Art. 12: "为了提高执法效率，给市场主体提供明确的预期 … ".

82 Commission Regulation (EU) 316/2014 of 21 March, 2014.

83 *Id.*, Art. 4 Sect. 1 (a) – (c).

84 Stephanie Wu, *China Publishes the 2nd Version of the Anti-Monopoly Guidelines on the Abuse of Intellectual Property Rights*, April 2017, CPI Competition Policy International, available at https://www.competitionpolicyinternational.com/wp-content/uploads/2017/04/Asia-Column-April-Full.pdf.

Guidelines stipulates that "*without justifiable reasons, a dominant under-taking, in particular if IPR is part of essential facility for production and business operations, refuses to license its IPR to other business operator, may constitute abuse of market dominance to exclude or restrict competi-tion.*" In addition, Art. 15 sets forth five factors which may be considered in assessing whether refusal to license IPR constitutes abusive conduct:

(1) commitment made by the business operator to license the IPR
(2) whether the IPR is indispensable for other business operators to enter the relevant market
(3) refusal to license such IPRs will result in negative effects and the de-gree of negative effects on innovation from other business operators
(4) whether the rejected licensee lacks will and capability to pay reason-able license fees
(5) whether refusal to license relevant IPRs will damage the interests of consumers and the public

3.1 The essential facility doctrine adopted by SAIC

In the current *Provisions* from SAIC, the essential facility doctrine was in-troduced in Art. 7. Upon examining and comparing the languages and adopted factors in SAIC's *Provisions* and Art. 15 of the Guidelines, one may conclude that Art. 15 introduced a much more cautious approach in assessing abusive conduct of refusal to deal. The wording "indispensable" in the above-mentioned factor (2) and "degree of negative effects" in fac-tor (3) did not appear in SAIC's *Provisions*. This more tentative attitude of the latest *IP Guidelines* on the essential facility doctrine could be the re-sult of heavy criticism directed at Art. 7 of SAIC's *Provisions* in 2015.

3.2 The essential facility doctrine from the US perspective

It is widely accepted that this doctrine was first developed in the US case *Terminal Railroad Association*[85] in 1912 ruled by the Supreme Court. However, in 2004 the US Supreme Court explicitly denied the existence of the essential facility doctrine in the *Trinko* case. *"We have never recog-*

---

85 *United States v. Terminal Railroad Association*, 224 U.S. 383 (1912).

nized such a doctrine...... We find no need either to recognize it or to repudiate it here. It suffices for present purposes to note that the indispensable requirement for invoking the doctrine is the unavailability of access to the 'essential facilities'; where access exists, the doctrine serves no purpose" In the US, the court generally observes that forced sharing may discourage the incentives for innovation which eventually will benefit consumers.[86]

A brief overview of the development of the US antitrust law may reflect its attitude towards the essential facility doctrine. The US federal antitrust law has developed over more than a century's time. The core part is found in the 1890 Sherman Act and the 1914 Clayton Act, which went through amendments over time. The refinement of the US antitrust law including its jurisprudence evolved with changes of the political and economic climate within the country. The adoption of the Sherman Act was the endorsement of the Congress for the free market principle. This general principle should contribute to the long-established ideals of economic opportunity, freedom of exchange, security of property and political liberty.[87] From another perspective, one may also understand that the US antitrust law was established in response to populist political pressure to curb large trusts' economic power and monopolization at the market.[88] By the 1970s, the US adjudication was strongly influenced by the Chicago School of antitrust economic theory on *efficiency*, which replaced the Harvard structuralism.[89] With the "law-and-economics" movement, the US courts tend to interpret the goals of the antitrust law much more narrowly based solely on economic theory.[90] The efficiency argument was readily accepted at

---

86 Maureen K. Ohlhausen, *Illuminating the Story of China's Anti-Monopoly Law*, October 2013, available at https://www.ftc.gov/sites/default/files/documents/public_statements/illuminating-story-chinas-anti-monopoly-law/1310amlstory.pdf.

87 James May, *Antitrust in the Formative Era: Political and Economic Theory in Constitutional and Antitrust Analysis, 1890-1918*, (1989) 50 Ohio State Law Journal 258 – 395; see also Qianlan Wu, *Competition Laws, Globalization and Legal Pluralism* (Hart Publishing Ltd. 2013) 17.

88 *Supra* note 44.

89 In examining the restraints on competition by merger, courts focus on impact on the market structure and if there would be market foreclosure, which will prevent other competitors from entering the relevant market. *Brown Shoe* decision by the Warren Court is a typically influenced by Harvard structuralism. See also Qianlan Wu, *Competition Laws, Globalization and Legal Pluralism*, (Hart Publishing Ltd. 2013) 18.

90 *Supra* note 44.

that time owing to fierce global competition, in particular from Japanese companies. The US antitrust law strongly advocates for efficiency, and belief in self-correction of the market.

3.3 The essential facility doctrine under the EU law

The development of essential facilities doctrine within the EU is widely believed to be a natural consequence of privatizing infrastructure and other public utility goods in order to break up the dominance of such companies.[91] In addition to tangible facilities such as public infrastructure, the European Court of Justice (ECJ) has made a series of rulings on intangible facilities involving IPRs. Most of the court decisions under the EU competition law are cases on refusal to deal rather than on essential facilities.[92] In the past decades, the EU case law established the criteria for "exceptional circumstance test" when assessing if a "refusal to deal" has competition implications or not. *Bronner* case[93] is widely taken as a turning point of EU's attitude towards this doctrine. In the ruling of this case the ECJ set higher standards than, for instance, on *Commercial Solvents* case[94]. The fact that the facility owner possesses a dominant market position is not sufficient for him to be ordered to deal with its competitors. In comparison with the view from the US Supreme Court, the ECJ accepted that in certain exceptional circumstances, a refusal to supply a potential competitor with an essential facility can constitute a breach of Article 82 of the EC Treaty.[95] The exceptional circumstances were first mentioned in the *Magill* case[96]. In this case, the abusive conduct resulted from the "refusal to

---

91 James Turney, *Defining the Limits of the EU Essential Facilities Doctrine on Intellectual Property Rights: The Primacy of Securing Optimal Innovation*, Northwestern Journal of Technology and Intellectual Property, 2005, Vol 3, No. 2.
92 Sebastien J. Evrard, *Essential Facilities in the European Union: Bronner and Beyond,* 10 Colum. J. Eur. L. 491 (2003-2004).
93 *Bronner v. Mediaprint*, C-7/97, [1998 E.C.R.] at I-7791.
94 *Commercial Solvents v. Commission*, C-7/73 [1974 E.C.R.] at 223.
95 CONSOLIDATED VERSIONS OF THE TREATY ON EUROPEAN UNION AND OF THE TREATY ESTABLISHING THE EUROPEAN COMMUNITY (2002), (2002/C 325/01), available at http://eur-lex.europa.eu/legal-content/EN/TXT/PDF/?uri=CELEX:12002E/TXT&from=EN.
96 *Radio Telefis Eireann (RTE) and Independent Television Publications Ltd (ITP) v. Commission,* Joined Cases C-241/91 P & C-242/91, P, 1995 E.C.R. I-743, [1995] 4 C.M.L.R.718.

deal" prevented emergence of a new product, namely a general television magazine which consumers require.

The *Microsoft* decision[97] in 2007 is another landmark case in the EU on competition law applying to intellectual property. The EU invoked competition rules for consumer welfare against absolute IP protection,[98] and imposed on *Microsoft* to release the interoperability code to its competitors. This case started with a complaint filed by *Sun Microsystems*, alleging that *Microsoft* refused to supply it with interoperability information for inter-operation with Microsoft's operating system. After examination the Commission held that Microsoft's interoperability code was indispensable for other operating systems to interoperate with Windows system. Furthermore, the refusal to license prevented other competitors to come up with new products in the relevant market which customers demand. Therefore, *Microsoft* abused its market dominance and its refusal to license constituted violation of Art. 82 EC.[99] In consistence with the decision of *Magill* case, the Court of First Instance affirmed the findings of the Commission.

From the EU jurisprudence, particularly from the *Microsoft* case ruling, it is apparent that the market structure and some equality for competitors should be maintained. However, the *Microsoft* decision triggered heavy debates in the relevant circles. Some argued that the Windows operating system has already become a *quasi* consumer standard and available at a very competitive price. The EU competition authorities nevertheless intervened based on Microsoft's strong market power and its imposition of unfair conditions upon other market participants.[100] One may conclude that under the EU competition policy and its general attitude toward essential facilities doctrine, a compulsory license is more likely to be granted for intangible facilities than under the US competition regime.

---

97 *Microsoft v. Commission*, T-201/04 (2007).

98 Tsenchov, *Latest Development in the Microsoft Case in the European Union: Microsoft Officially Allows Browser Choice to Customers*, (2010), The Columbia Journal of European Law 16, page 85 – 88.

99 Art. 82 EC corresponds to Art. 102 TFEU.

100 *Supra* note 91.

3.4 Compulsory license under TRIPs Agreement

Under TRIPs Agreement general framework is laid down in various stipulations. Art. 8(2) of TRIPs Agreement gives member states a general guidance that appropriate measures may be introduced in each country's own legislation to prevent abuse of IPRs. Article 31 of the Agreement sets forth clear provisions, under which a compulsory license can be granted once the judicial or administrative review establishes anti-competitive conduct of IPR holders.

Furthermore, Art. 40(1) acknowledges that some licensing practices of IPRs may have adverse effects on trade, and may impede the transfer and dissemination of technology. Art. 40(2) specifies examples of anti-competitive practice such as exclusive grant-back conditions, preventing challenges to validity and coercive package licensing. These are also focal points of the Chinese IP Guidelines concerning licensing practice, which will be discussed below.

3.5 Inevitable legal uncertainty of the essential facility doctrine

As elaborated earlier, it can become a complex task to strike the right balance between IPR protection and competition policy. Courts from older jurisdictions such as the EU and the US have to carefully weigh the balance between the interest of IPR holders and consumer benefits irrespective of whether the essential facilities doctrine is explicitly recognised or not. In the case of intangible essential facilities, unlike with tangible essential facilities such as harbours or airports, the investment put into innovations and new ideas cannot be easily measured. And precisely for further promoting such creativity, exclusive IPR regime exists to protect inventors. Innovation will be hampered, if the exclusivity is taken away from innovators through an "easy" compulsory license based on essential facility doctrine. Because of the great difficulties to reconcile the two regimes, it is almost impossible for regulators to set up a clear rule for limiting exclusivity of IPR holders for the benefit of overall consumer welfare. This requires competition agencies and courts to take decisions on a case-by-case basis.

Based on the wording of the *IP Guidelines*, it is assumed that the Chinese authorities would take similar cautious approaches in assessing if a compulsory license should be granted. For emerging economies, it might be quite tempting to apply this doctrine, since certain patented technologies may not yet be available in the country. Any lax application of the doctrine by granting compulsory license would discourage the incentives of innovators. Art. 15 of the *IP Guidelines* somewhat reflects the cautious attitude of the Chinese regulators. It still remains to be seen how competition agencies will put this newly introduced doctrine into practice, and how future judicial judgements would further interpret the principle. Any legal uncertainty is problematic, since recoupment of innovations could be jeopardized simply by an order to license their IPRs to a competitor.[101]

4. SEP licensing

The whole Chapter 2 (Articles 6 to 12) of the *IP Guidelines* deals with IP-related monopoly agreements. Articles 6 to 10 specify the following conducts: joint R&D, cross-license, exclusive grant-back, non-challenge clause, standard setting. All these articles have also close relationships with SEP licensing.

As will be discussed in Part V, standard essential patents (SEP) could grant patent holders automatic access to downstream product markets by licensing the standard technology. In spite of the dynamic efficiency and the possible *ex post* effect of innovation for dynamic industries, licensors do have stronger bargaining power than licensees. Particularly at this stage, a large number of Chinese companies are licensees. Therefore, Chinese policy-makers and competition authorities have reasons to pay close attention to fair licensing practice involving SEPs.

The message from the provisions in Chapter 2 and the pertinent factors to be considered is quite clear. Incentives of innovation from licensees should not be discouraged and hampered by coercions from the licensor. Art. 8 of the *IP Guidelines* concerns only exclusive grant-backs. Factors to be considered are, *inter alia,* whether licensor provides substantial values for the exclusive grant-backs, or whether the exclusive grant-backs discourage licensee to innovate. In order to motivate licensee to further develop the licensed technology, it is detrimental to bind licensees with certain obligations and terms such as free granting back the improved licensed technology to the licensor, or "non-challenging clauses" of patent

---

101 *Supra* note 91.

validity. These conducts are also explicitly put as "excluded restrictions" in Art. 5 Section 1(a) and (b) of the TTBER Regulation.[102] The deep concern on technology licensing agreement of the Chinese policy-makers seems to be fully in line with the approach of the EU. This demonstrates the importance of maintaining licensee's incentives to further develop and diffuse technology, which is the very essence of both IPR regime and competition policy.[103]

C. Some Concluding Remarks

The release of the long-awaited *IP Guidelines* will provide IP owners with certainty and predictability when exercising their IPRs in China. The validity of the Guidelines will apply to all three competition agencies in China.

The long drafting process and repeated amendments signaled that the intersection between exclusivity of IPR and the competition regime is extremely delicate. With the *IP Guidelines* Chinese competition authorities seek to provide principles and examining criteria to distinguish between permissible business practice and abuse of IPRs. As discussed above, there still cannot be a very clear demarcation between the two systems. Future administrative and judicial decisions will contribute to establishment of clearer rules. A few aspects of *IP Guidelines* need to be improved. As an example, further clarifications on terms such as essential facilities would be of great help. According to the EU experience, only if other market participants are hindered to compete in a downstream market, should the doctrine be instituted.

Furthermore, in various provisions, though a list of factors for determining abuse of IP rights is given for assessment purposes, the language sometimes sounds rather ambiguous. It would be commendable to the Chinese authorities to give weight to each mentioned factor according to its significance so that more predictability can be established.

Clearly, the draft *IP Guidelines* intend to provide adequate protection for licensees. In this aspect, US commentators urged the Chinese authorities to reconsider provisions such as non-challenge clause and expired and

---

102 See Commission Regulation (EU) No 316/2014 of 21 March 2014.

103 *Supra* note 4.

invalid patents in package licensing portfolios. They should not be regarded as inherently or likely anti-competitive.[104]

It is important for younger jurisdictions like China to borrow doctrines that have already been given interpretations in older jurisdictions. This will generally speaking increase predictability for market participants. In this sense, it is even more essential for Chinese competition agencies and courts to consistently and tentatively apply those newly introduced doctrines.

---

104 Melisa Lipman, *Antitrust Group Urges China to Adjust Approach to IP Abuse*, Available at https://www.law360.com/articles/913654/antitrust-group-urges-china-to-adjust-approach-to-ip-abuse.

V. Competition Policy and IPRs: Well-Functioning Symbiosis – A Case Study

A. Brief Introduction to SEP and Related Issues

In our daily life we take it for granted that "telephones talk to each other, the Internet works, and hairdryers plug into electrical sockets because private groups have set 'interface' standards, allowing compatibility between products made by different manufacturers."[105] A standard can be defined as a set of technical specifications that seeks to provide a common design for a product or process.[106] Without standards, we would have to buy different telephones whenever we travel to a different country or even to different regions in the same country. Standards will ensure interoperability of products from different manufacturers that are fundamental for consumers to save costs. Standards also promote quality, utility, safety, and foster competition among different producers for the benefits of consumers.

To ensure compatibility of different manufacturers' products, industry groups negotiate and agree on technical standards. These are standard setting organisations (SSOs).[107] The chosen technology should be the most suitable for that specific sector and will be incorporated in the industry, be it mechanical, electrical, chemical or telecommunication-related sectors. Implementing a standard may require use of a patented technology. Wherever a standard requires use of patented technology, this patent is called standard essential patents (SEPs).[108] An SEP holder may take advantage of his unique position and try to gain more market shares by exploiting his

---

105 Mark. A. Lemley, *Intellectual Property Rights & Standard-Setting Organizations*, 90 Cal, L. Rev. 1889, 1893 (2002).

106 H. Hovenkamp et al., *IP and Antitrust: An Analysis of Antitrust Principles Applied to Intellectual Property Law*, Sect. 35.1 (Supp.2003-04).

107 Steven M. Amundson, *Recent Decisions Provide Some Clarity on How Courts and Government Agencies Will Likely Resolve Issues Involving Standard-Essential Patents,* Chicago-Kent Journal of Intellectual Property, Vol. 13 (2013).

108 *Apple, Inc. v. Motorola Mobility, Inc.* 886 F. Supp.2d 1061, 1067 (W.D. Wis. 2012).

SEP to exclude others. In addition, SEP holder may impose higher royalty fees on licensees. This exploitation is named as patent hold-up.[109]

In recent years, patent hold-up problems in telecommunication industry appeared to be rampant, whereby competition policy was supposed to provide countermeasures. However, the situation is more complex than one can imagine. Studies demonstrated that damages payable to implementers solving the patent hold-up problem can restore their stimulus to invest. But this in turn would reduce innovators' incentives to carry on R&D and thus discourage further innovation.[110] In addition, complicated technologies, multitude of patent protections and fragmented ownership of SEPs in this field exacerbate the complexity. Hence, how to balance and optimize the interests of both parties has become a real challenge for competition enforcers.

Like in other major jurisdictions in the world, Chinese competition authorities have similar concerns on patent hold-up problems. Since the enactment of the Chinese Anti-Monopoly Law (AML) in 2008, both administrative and judicial competition authorities have been involved in applying competition law to the abuse of standard essential patents.

Besides the *Huawei* case which will be discussed more in-depth below, it is worth mentioning another landmark decision issued by China's competition agency NDRC - the *Qualcomm* decision. As a reminder, this company was abusing its dominant market position and charging Chinese mobile device producers excessively high royalty prices upon licensing its SEPs. Other unfair conditions such as bundling of SEPs with non-SEPs, charging royalties for invalid patents, royalty free granting-back were also found after fifteen months of investigation into the company. NDRC fined *Qualcomm* USD 975 million, which is the highest amount ever imposed upon a single company by Chinese competition authorities. The major findings of Qualcomm's abusive conduct for licensing its SEPs is reflected in the latest guidelines for applying AML to IPRs, which was discussed in Part IV.

In a globalized economy anticompetitive conduct in China will not only impact Chinese consumers, but also consumers in other parts of the world.

---

109 Joseph Farrell et al., *Standard Setting, Patents & Hold-up*, 74 Antitrust Law Journal 603, 603-04 (2007).

110 Bernhard Ganglmair, et al., *Patent Hold-up and Antitrust: How a Well-Intentioned Rule Could Retard Innovation*, The Journal of Industrial Economics, Vol LX, June (2012).

In the following, *Huawei v. InterDigital* - another landmark decision taken by the Chinese courts on the intersection between competition regime and IPR will be elaborated.

B. *Judicial Decision on Huawei v. InterDigital*

1. Case outline

InterDigital Technology Corporation, Inc. (IDC) is an American company headquartered in Delaware. *IDC* as a group designs and develops advanced technologies for wireless communications, and owned more than 19 500 patent and patent applications worldwide at the time of the lawsuit in December 2011. Numerous patents in its portfolio were SEPs. *IDC* had participated in the formulation of international wireless communication standards.

Huawei Technologies Co., Ltd. (Huawei), based in Shenzhen, China, is the largest manufacturer of telecommunication devices in the world. Its products are exported to more than 170 countries and regions.[111] *Huawei* serves almost all of the world's largest telecom operators, and among others Huawei implements SEPs for wireless technologies from *IDC*.

Both companies are members of the European Telecommunications Standardisation Institute (ETSI). According to Art. 6.1 of ETSI Intellectual Property Rights Policy[112], once patents are declared standard essential patents, it is mandatory for members to grant irrevocable licenses on fair, reasonable, and non-discrimination (FRAND) conditions.

On December 5, 2011, *Huawei* filed two lawsuits against *IDC* at Shenzhen Intermediate People's Court (Shenzhen Court). In the first complaint (case 857)[113] *Huawei* asked for a judicial ruling on the level of royalties for certain patents to be paid by *Huawei* to *IDC*. In the second complaint (case 858)[114] Huawei alleged that *IDC* had abused its dominant market position pursuant to Art. 17 of the AML, and *IDC* failed to negotiate on

---

111 See Annual Report of Huawei, 2016, available at http://www.huawei.com/en/about-huawei/annual-report/2016/foreword.
112 *ETSI Intellectual Property Rights Policy*, April 5, 2017, available at http://www.etsi.org/images/files/IPR/etsi-ipr-policy.pdf.
113 Shen Zhong Fa Zhi Min Chu Zi No. 857 [2011], 深中法知民初字第 857 号.
114 Shen Zhong Fa Zhi Min Chu Zi No. 858 [2011], 深中法知民初字第 858 号.

FRAND terms when licensing its SEPs for wireless communication technologies. *IDC* should compensate Huawei RMB 20 million in damages.

It should be noted that earlier, in July 2011 *IDC* had filed a patent infringement litigation against *Huawei* at Delaware District Court, alleging that the defendant infringed IDC's patents and asked for preliminary injunction and damages. In addition, *IDC* filed patent infringement litigation against *Huawei* with the US International Trade Commission (ITC), requesting for prohibition from import and sales in the USA.

2. Substantial rulings of the Chinese courts

Both decisions regarding cases 857 and 858 from the Shenzhen Court were appealed to Guangdong Higher People's Court (Guangdong High Court), which made the final judgement in October 2013.[115] The appellate court affirmed the ruling from the Shenzhen Court. The judgement from the Shenzhen Court can be summarized as follows.

2.1 IDC holds a dominant position

Pursuant to Article 12 of the AML and Articles 3 and 4 of the *Guideline*[116] relevant geographic and product markets need to be determined first. Shenzhen Court first defined the relevant product market to be each SEP licensing market for 3G technology standards (WCMA, CDMA2000, and TD-SCDMA). The relevant geographic markets were China and the US. The Shenzhen Court further analysed the interchangeability and possible substitutability of the respective technologies. The Shenzhen Court made the conclusion that due to the uniqueness and non-substitutability of each SEP for implementers, *IDC* possesses 100 percent market share regarding WCMA, CDMA2000, and TD-SCDMA standards for 3G telecommunications technology. Therefore, *IDC* holds without any doubt a dominant position. Guangdong High Court affirmed the market definitions in its published decision.

---

115 Guangdong High People's Court, Yue Gao Fa Min San Zhong Zi No. 306 [2013], 粤高法民三终字第 306 号.

116 *Supra* note 72.

2.2 Abuse of dominant position in licensing SEP technology

Pursuant to the AML, dominant position alone does not constitute a violation of the law. Abusive conduct of the dominant market power must be proved. Based on the documents placed before the Shenzhen Court, it was concluded that *IDC* abuses its dominant position because of the following conduct

– Seeking injunctive relief before the US District Court of Delaware and the ITC *during* the negotiations with Huawei and thereby breaching the FRAND commitment
– requiring Huawei to pay much higher royalties than those paid by Apple and Samsung
– tying its SEPs with non-SEPs during licensing negotiations

The Shenzhen Court ruled that *IDC* abused its dominant market position, and should compensate *Huawei* RMB 20 million in damages.

With respect to case No. 857 the Shenzhen Court ruled that the royalty rate payable to *IDC* by *Huawei* should be reduced from 2 percent to 0.019 percent of actual sales price of each product produced by *Huawei*. With this ruling, Shenzhen Court became the very first court in China to determine a FRAND royalty rate. On appeal, the decision from the Shenzhen Court was affirmed by Guangdong High Court.

The court decisions triggered heated debates in the international community. While the Supreme People's Court praised the judgement as one of the "benchmark" cases, the US Chamber of Commerce critised the ruling very strongly and highlighted various irregularities.[117] The major findings of the ruling will now be examined.

3. Comments on main findings of the Chinese courts

It should be noted that out of confidentiality reasons, information about the rulings from the Shenzhen Court was made available only through numerous press release and publicized comments made by relevant judges

---

117 Critics such as poor reasoning of the judgement, competence of jurisdiction of the courts, etc. were raised. See US Chamber of Commerce, *Competing interests in China's Competition Law Enforcement: China's Anti-Monopoly Law Application and the Role of Industrial Policy*, page 75.

and attorneys involved in the case. But the judgement from Guangdong High Court was disclosed, with sensitive information barred.

3.1 Definition of market dominance by Guangdong High Court

The high court affirmed the conclusion of Shenzhen Court on market definition. Detailed analysis was given in the ruling on definition of geographical and product markets. The definition of product market is decisive here in order to determine market dominance concerning the specific product. In this regard the Guangdong High Court adopted similar approaches as set in the Commission Notice on the Definition of the Relevant Market, in that the interchangeability and substitutability of relevant technologies were carefully analysed. The Court spent lengthy part explaining the characteristics of SEP, which factually forces implementers to seek licenses from the SEP proprietor. In other words, the SEP owner becomes the only supplier of that standard and thus, there is no substitute in the relevant market.

In this context, one needs to be aware of the consequences if a narrower relevant market has been established. The IPR holder tends to be confronted with a domino effect which subsequently leads to reduced possibilities of identifying substitutes in a narrow market. This would even result in a single product market[118], as we can see from the above case. Under such circumstances, a strong market power and dominant position is automatically established.[119]

In the recent ruling from the European Court of Justice (ECJ) on *Huawei v. ZTE* case, however, the Advocate General Melchior Wathelet stated that "... *the fact that an undertaking owns an SEP does not necessarily mean that it holds a dominant position within the meaning of Art. 102 TFEU...*".[120] It seems that the ECJ applied a more careful approach upon assessing dominant position of an SEP holder. It is definitely advisable to examine all the relevant circumstances and the specific context of a case. Market dominance should be evaluated and determined on a

---

118 Steven Andermann and Hedvig Schmidt: *EU competitioin law and IPR, the regulation of innovation* (2nd edition, Oxford Uni Press, 2011), 45 – 46.

119 *Id.*

120 *Huawei Technologies Co. Ltd. v. ZTE Corp, ZTE Deutschland GmbH,* C-170/13, , [2014] [57].

case-by-case basis. It is not easy to find a middle way to avoid either under-protection or over-protection of an SEP owner. In recent years, a series of decisions in major jurisdictions around the world might give the impression that SEP holders are under-protected. Large amount of penalties have been imposed on various SEP and IPR owners, particularly in the field of telecommunication and software. For instance, *Qualcomm* was fined USD 975 million in 2015 by the Chinese competition authority NDRC.[121] The Korean Fair Trade Commission (KFTC) imposed another penalty on *Qualcomm* in the amount of USD 854 million in December 2016.[122] In another case, the EU Commission imposed a penalty payment of Euro 899 million on *Microsoft* for non-compliance with the Commission's decision in 2004.[123]

3.2 Abuse of dominant position

Based on the evidential materials, the Guangdong High Court found that *IDC* had sought injunctive relief at the Delaware Court and with the ITC to prohibit *Huawei* from using its SEPs during the negotiation process. Injunctions sought in the US against a willing licensee would eliminate and restrict export activities of *Huawei* with the purpose of imposing unfairly high licensing terms. Hence, *IDC* abused its dominant position by breaching the FRAND commitment.

The above ruling seems to be in line with decisions on similar cases in the EU. In the European Commission decision on *Motorola Mobility*[124] released in April 2014, it was stated that *Motorola Mobility* filed lawsuit against *Apple* in Germany based on an SEP, although the latter was willing

---

121 *Administrative Sanction Decision from National Development and Reform Commission of People's Republic of China* (中华人民共和国国家发展和改革委员会行政处罚决定书), February 9, 2015, available at http://www.ndrc.gov.cn/gzdt/201503/t20150302_666209.html.

122 Global 500 Reuters News, December 28, 2016, available at http://fortune.com/2016/12/27/qualcomm-korea-antitrust/.

123 European Commission Press Release, February 27, 2008, available at http://europa.eu/rapid/press-release_IP-08-318_en.htm.

124 European Commission Press Release, *Antitrust: Commission finds that Motorola Mobility infringed EU competition rules by misusing standard essential patents*, April 29, 2014, available at http://europa.eu/rapid/press-release_IP-14-489_en.htm.

to enter a license agreement. According to the Commission *"Seeking injunction before courts is generally a legitimate remedy for patent holders in case of patent infringements. However, the seeking of an injunction based on SEPs may constitute an abuse of a dominant position if an SEP holder has given a voluntary commitment to license its SEPs on FRAND terms and where the company against which an injunction is sought is willing to enter into a licence agreement on such FRAND terms."*

The lawsuit brought by *IDC* at the Delaware District Court and ITC could indeed distort the negotiations process and would lead to anti-competitive licensing terms which could be detrimental to innovation and to the interests of consumers.

3.3 Chinese court sets the royalty rate

Can a court adjudicate pure commercial matters such as royalty level under the circumstances that there is no tort or no breach of contract? In this case, the plaintiff complained about the much higher rate to be paid to *IDC* in comparison with the payable royalties by *Apple* or *Samsung*. Evidential documents showed that the royalty rate to be paid by *Huawei* for the same set of patents would have been nineteen times higher than that paid by *Apple*, and two times higher than that paid by *Samsung*.[125] The Shenzhen Court stated that judicial remedy had to be sought because two parties could not reach an agreement and *IDC* had breached its commitment to licensing the SEPs under FRAND terms.

As to the level of royalties, the Shenzhen Court provided the factors to be considered such as relevant situation in the industry, quantity, quality and value of IDC's SEPs. Decision on a concrete figure was taken pursuant to Art. 4 of the General Principles of the Civil Law, and Art. 5 and 6

---

125 Li Hui, *Rethinking the Competition Case, Huawei Wins the Lawsuit against IDC* (还原华为反 IDC 垄断案，胜诉背后的反思). The following information was revealed by Huawei's attorney: IDC singed with Apple a global licensing agreement on 3G-patents. Licensing term lasted 7 years which started from June 2007. The licensing fee was in the amount of USD 56 million. IDC's global licensing agreement with Samsung for its 2G and 3G-patents was signed in 2009 and would last for 4 years. Total amount was USD 400 million. For comparable patents IDC asked Huawei to pay USD 1.5 billion. September 29, 2015, available at http://www.maxlaw.cn/l/20150929/830281649635.shtml.

of the Contract Law.[126] However, according to InterDigital's Securities and Exchange Commission filings, the Chinese court failed to provide explanations.[127]

In fact, the Chinese court was not the only one which has set the level of royalty rate. *In the Microsoft v. Motorola* case, the US District Court Western District of Washington at Seattle also set the licensing rate for Motorola's video coding SEP portfolio to *Microsoft*. In the summary judgement from February 27, 2012, Judge Jame L. Robart stated that "... *the court believes that reasonable parties may disagree as to the terms and conditions of a (F)RAND license, leaving the courthouse as the only viable arena to determine the meaning of "reasonable" under the circumstances.*"[128]

3.4 SEP-related controversies

A standard can be defined as a set of technical specifications that seeks to provide a common design for a product or process.[129] Industrial history is filled with examples of rivals agreeing on product standardization for reasons of utility, safety, or cartelization.

Standardization will almost always have some advantages for consumers. Industry-wide compliance to standards is crucial to growth and efficiency. Generally speaking only the best and the most efficient solutions will be adopted as standards. The aggregate positive effect for the economy is significant, and consumers should finally benefit from standards. However, once a standard is adopted, it is not possible to manufacture products that comply with a certain standard without accessing these patents. This may confer significant market power on companies holding SEPs. The consequences would be that standard implementers need a license from the standard holders, who own patents on standard technologies. In the decision on *Huawei v. IDC*, the Guangdong High Court em-

---

126 Guangliang Zhang et al., *A Review of Huawei v. IDC*, Managing Intellectual Property, March 27, 2015, available at http://www.managingip.com/Article/3440420/A-review-of-Huawei-v-IDC.html.

127 InterDigital 10-Q report, filed October 31, 2013, available at http://www.snl.com/Cache/c34365872.html.

128 *Microsoft Corporation v. Motorola, Inc., et al.*, C10-1823JLR (2012).

129 H. Hovenkamp et al: *IP and Antitrust: An Analysis of Antitrust Principles Applied to Intellectual Property Law*; Sect. 35.1 (Supp. 2003 -04).

phasised that *"the monopolistic power conferred by the patent regime is greatly strengthened due to the mandatory character of the technology standard"*.

The general concern regarding the "locked-in" effect caused by a standard to which an implementer chooses to adhere was clearly delineated in the ruling on *Broadcom v. Qualcomm* case. *"Industry participants who have invested significant resources developing products and technologies that conform to the standard will find it **prohibitively expensive**[130] to abandon their investment and switch to another standard. They will have become "locked in" to the standard. In this unique position of bargaining power, the patent holder may be able to extract supra competitive royalties from the industry participants."*[131]

As elaborated above, SEP owners as licensors indeed possess more bargaining power vis-à-vis licensees and can thereby impose excessive high royalties and more favourable conditions for themselves. Particularly in telecommunications we see giant companies like *Qualcomm*, *Samsung* and *InterDigital* with a huge patent portfolio. It is noteworthy that *InterDigial* has no production, and licensing business is the only source of its revenues. It is also common knowledge that *Qualcomm's* licensing business is far more profitable than earnings from manufacturing the chipsets. Yet, it is fair to say that the *ex post* benefit of becoming a "trend-setter" drives companies to invest a huge amount of their capital in innovation. The *ex ante* sunk capital in research can barely be numbered. This needs to be taken into account by competition enforcers when assessing anticompetitive conduct.

Adoption of a technological standard *automatically* grants SEP owners access to downstream markets. Their market power conferred by patent law is therefore extended via licensing agreement with the implementers. While manufacturers and implementers are trapped in the standard, SEP holders may start to put pressure on licensees and try to impose their terms and conditions. Most SSOs have rules to curb this problem and generally require their members to commit to licensing SEPs on FRAND terms. This commitment is meant to ensure access to standards for all market participants to prevent hold-up by a single SEP owner. In spite of the

---

130 Emphasis added.
131 *Broadcom Corp. v. Qualcomm Inc.*, [2007], 501 F. 3d 297.

above, the number of litigations on FRAND licensing terms is constantly increasing in major jurisdictions worldwide.

Patent hold-up issues may also cause royalty stacking problem. This is partly due to expansion and strengthening of IPR protection. More importantly, the complexity of an advanced technology requires incorporation of a multitude of complementary technologies. The patent system creates a sort of *patent ticket*, whereby an overlapping set of patents forces market participants seeking to commercialize new technologies to obtain licenses from multiple patentees.[132] Standard adoption process by which cooperative standards are typically set, and the *ex post* potential of anti-competitive market power conferred on SEP holders may indeed lead to controversial situations. Taking smart phones as an example, Lemley and Shapiro stated that they had "seen estimates [for W-CDMA] as high as 30 percent of the total prices of each phone… based on summing royalty demands before any cross-licensing negotiations began."[133] Even according to a more conservative estimate, cumulative royalties for GSM for companies not possessing any patents to trade stood at 10-13 percent.[134] The terms and conditions in a licensing agreement between SEP owners and licensees will eventually impact consumes interests.

The above discussions were concentrated on the downstream market. But this is only one side of the story. Companies invest large amounts of capital in R&D before their pioneering technologies can be incorporated in the standard. Only if innovators can recoup their investment, will they take further risks and engage in further technological development. Sufficient protection should be accorded to innovators, which is the very purpose of patent regime. Recent studies on upstream markets revealed a few interesting aspects. The main interest of standard owner is to constantly upgrade standards so that a complete replacement becomes difficult. This can result in large numbers of patent portfolios building around the stan-

---

132 Carl Shapiro, *"Navigating the Patent Thicket: Cross Licenses, Patent Pools, and Standards Setting"*, in Adam B. Jaffe, Josh Lerner and Scott Stern (eds), *Innovation Policy and the Economy*, Vol. 1, MIT Press, 2001.

133 *Id.*

134 Eric Stasik: *Royalty Rates and Licensing Strategies For Essential Patents On LTE (4G) Telecommunication Standards*; Royalty rates for Telecommunications, September 2010.

dard.[135] The other side of the coin is that standard implementers do not need to have excessive concerns about the "locked-in" effect of their sunk investment in developing complementary products and other commercialization activities.[136] Empirical experience shows that discontinuation and replacement of the set standard does not take place very often.

Furthermore, a single owner of SEPs is apparently in a better position to internalize returns from essential patents, or acting as platform leader to promote and sponsor the relevant standard. Fragmented ownership of SEPs encourages free-riding and decreases incentives of further investment by the standard setters.[137] In addition to the aforementioned points, it is also important to keep the specific characteristics in the new economy in mind. Emergence of giant companies and dominant market shares of one player is also owed to the natural consequence of the "network" effect, which characterizes our digitally interconnected environment. In the *Microsoft* decision in 2007, the European Commission seems to be skeptical of the network effects prevalent in the new economy and regard it as an unjustifiable barrier to entry. There are arguments that artificially fragmenting the market will likely damage the efficiency of the industry and ultimately consumers have to bear the costs.[138]

The above findings have important implications for competition agencies and judicial bodies. In order to properly instate the competition law as a countermeasure against abuse of IP right, it is vital to recognize dynamic efficiency brought by innovation in certain high-tech industries. We all acknowledge that innovation should be promoted, but it is difficult to make judgement on future welfare effects for the society. Enforcers could apply the concept of *dynamic competition* relying on facts that characterize competition in the relevant markets.[139] "This approach enables competition law enforcers to apply an *ex post* assessment to the greatest extent possi-

---

135 Justus Baron et al., *Essential Patent and Standard Dynamics*, March 15, 2013, available at https://www.law.northwestern.edu/research-faculty/searlecenter/innovationeconomics/documents/Essential_Patents_and_Standard_Dynamics_2013.pdf.

136 *Id.*

137 *Id.*

138 *Supra* note 91.

139 Josef Drexl: *Is there a 'more economic approach' to intellectual property and competition law?* Research Handbook on Intellectual Property and Competition Law, (Edward Elgar Publishing 2008) 40.

ble".[140] In summary, advanced technologies have posed competition authorities a formidable task. New analytical approaches need to be adopted when assessing IP-related anticompetitive conduct.

C. Possible Ways Ahead

The judicial decision on *Huawei v. InterDigital* is one of the landmark decisions on interface between competition policy and intellectual property. This case touched upon various issues such as definition of product market, abuse of dominant position and SEP licensing under FRAND terms. Furthermore, Shenzhen Court marks the first Chinese judicial body setting a royalty rate for licensing practice.

The definition of product market in this case seems to be in line with international practice, which also found reflections in the decision on *Qualcomm* issued by NDRC in 2015. As stated in the judgement from Guangdong High Court, there is deep concern on the extended market power possessed by an SEP holder. However, the level of royalty rate set by the court, which was rather low, might also impact Chinese SEP holders such as *Huawei* and *ZTE*. As to the breach of FRAND commitment, it would have been necessary for the courts to carefully evaluate which party was responsible for the failure of negotiations. Because this point was vital for determining the abuse of dominant position, detailed reasoning should have been presented by the courts. Yet, in the judgement there were only general findings that court proceedings had been initiated by *InterDigital* during the negotiation process.

Furthermore, controversy on industrial policy concern was aroused by the statements from the Chief Judge of the second instance court:

> *"Huawei's success in the anti-monopoly lawsuit is quite meaningful. Qiu Yongqing, the Chief Judge of the Guangdong Higher People's Court believes that Huawei's strategy of using anti-monopoly law as a countermeasure is worth learning by other Chinese enterprises. Qiu suggests that Chinese enterprises should bravely employ anti-monopoly lawsuits to break technology barriers and win space for development"*[141]

---

140 *Id.*

141 He Linping, et al, *Monopoly Dispute: Chinese Enterprise Won against American Giant* (垄断纠纷：中国企业打败美国巨头)，available at http://news.163.com/13/1028/21/9CA9N4JN00014JB6.html.

It is the goal of the Chinese government to encourage development of advanced technologies and to make China a strong IP country. With increasing awareness of applying competition law to abuse of IP rights in China, it could be expected that more enforcement actions on the interplay between competition policy and IPR will occur in the future.

Apart from all the above, this case also illustrates certain inherent conflicts between standard setters and standard implementers. The increasing number of litigations in the telecommunication field worldwide is indicative that FRAND obligations set by most SSOs may not be sufficient. The concern on *ex post* market power conferred by SEPs and the unpredictability of costs for standard implementers partly lies in the unpredictable nature of licensing fees.[142] Maybe it is time to consider additional *ex ante* binding commitment for standard setters.

---

142 Damien Geradin et al., *The Logic and Limits of ex ante Competition in a Standard-Setting Environment,* Competition Policy International, Vol. 3, No. 1, 2007.

VI. Conclusions

Competition law intends to protect the process of competition from restraints in the market by regulating the conduct of market participants. The adoption of the Anti-Monopoly Law by the Chinese government in 2008 was a natural result of China's economic transition from a centrally-planned economy to a market-oriented economic system.

This paper examines the Chinese experience in learning and devising its own competition regime in the context of a globalized world. The fact that the Chinese competition law took the European competition regime as major reference shows that a spectrum of factors including socio-economic, political and cultural elements plays an important role in formulating a competition regime. Precisely due to the influence coming from various other aspects of society, certain obstacles related to effective enforcement of the law cannot be tackled by the competition legislation alone. It is agreed among Chinese competition authorities and governmental officials that China needs to move further away from a planned economy. Undisputedly, more daring economic and political reforms will also ensure effectiveness of the competition law. To this end, administrative monopoly is one of the major barriers China needs to overcome.

Competition laws usually set general principles which are to be interpreted and implemented by administrative and judicial enforcement bodies. Depending on the perspective of viewpoint, which is also related to the level of economic and technological development, perceptions of competition can be rather different. As demonstrated in this study, concerns on competition issues in China find their concrete reflections not only in the statutory language of the AML and its implementing rules, but also in court decisions. Though strongly aligned to international rules and doctrines, China's latest draft *IP Guidelines* under the AML seek to develop their own principles by introducing elements that are strategically important for upgrading technological standards. For leading economies like China, adequate promotion of indigenous innovations is a vital concern.

In a globalized world, China's competition regime cannot be isolated from international legal norms. However, given China's economic weight, the success of introduction and implementation of a competition law with its own characteristics may set an example for other developing countries.

Regular BRICS International Competition Law Conferences offer an excellent platform for promoting thoughts, values and rules that are essential for high-growth economies. Some of these ideas might in fact have positive reverse impact on more mature jurisdictions.

History shows that competition law has its own dynamics and evolves over time. Future development of competition law should be based on better understanding of different cultural environments and their history in order to achieve more effective coordination and convergence.

List of Works Cited

Books

Andermann S. and Schmidt H., *EU competitioin law and IPR, the regulation of innovation* (2nd edition, Oxford Uni Press, 2011).

Drexl J. *Research Handbook on Intellectual Property and Competition Law* (Edward Elgar 2008)

Gerber D., *Law and Competition in Twentieth Century Europe: Protecting Prometheus* (Oxford University Press 1998)

Green C. and Rosenthal D., *Competition Regulation in the Pacific Rim* (Oceana Publications 1996)

He H., Zhao Fei, Qiao Xiaoyong et al., *Research on Anti-Monopolies in China* (Beijing Institute of Technology Press 2010)

Möschel W, "Competition Policy from an Ordo Point of View", A Peacock and H Willgerodt (eds.), *German Neo-Liberals and the Social Market Economy* (Macmillan 1989)

Sauter W., *Competition Law and Industrial Policy in the EU* (Oxford University Press 1997)

Shapiro C., "Navigating the Patent Thicket: Cross Licenses, Patent Pools, and Standards Setting", in Adam B. Jaffe, Josh Lerner and Scott Stern (eds.), Innovation Policy and the Economy, Vol. 1, MIT Press, 2001.

Wang X., "China's Competition Law in the Global Competition" in Nicolas Charbit, Elisa Ramundo (eds.), *Competition Law on the Global Stage: David Gerber's Global Competition Law in Perspective* (Institute of Competition Law 2014)

Wu Q., *Competition Laws, Globalization and Legal Pluralism, China's Experience* (Hart Publishing 2013)

Zhang H., *An Economic Analysis of China's Anti-Monopoly Law* (ProQuest 2011)

Monographies and Articles

Amundson S., "Recent Decisions Provide Some Clarity on How Courts and Government Agencies Will Likely Resolve Issues Involving Standard-Essential Patents", *Chicago-Kent Journal of Intellectual Property*, (2013) Vol. 13.

Broadman H., "Meeting the Challenge of Chinese Enterprise Reform" (1995) *World Bank*

Evrard S. J., "Essential Facilities in the European Union: Bronner and Beyond" (2003-2004) *10 Colum. J. Eur. L.*

Farrell J. et al., "Standard Setting, Patents & Hold-up", (2007) 74 *Antitrust Law Journal*

Ganglmair B. et al. "Patent Hold-up and Antitrust: How a Well-Intentioned Rule Could Retard Innovation" (2012) *The Journal of Industrial Economics*, Vol LX

Geradin D. et al. "The Logic and Limits of ex ante Competition in a Standard-Setting Environment" (2007) *Competition Policy International*" Vol. 3, No. 1

Gerber D. J., "Constructing Competition Law in China: The Potential Value of European and U.S. Experience" (2004) *Washington University Global Studies Law Review*

Kovacic W. E., "The United States and Its Future Influence on Global Competition Policy" (2015) *George Mason Law Review* 1157 – 1204.

Kovacic W. E., "Dominance, Duopoly and Oligopoly: The United States and the Development of Global Competition Policy" (2010) *Global Competition Review*

Koacic W. E., "Institutional Foundations for Economic Legal Reform in Transition Economies: The case of Competition Policy and Antitrust Enforcement" (2001) 77 *Chicago-Kent Law Review* 265.

Lemley M. A., "Intellectual Property Rights & Standard-Setting Organizations" (2002) 90 *Cal, L. Rev.* 1889, 1893.

May J., "Antitrust in the Formative Era: Political and Economic Theory in Constitutional and Antitrust Analysis" (1989) 50 *Ohio State Law Journal* 258 – 395

Nie P., "China's First Anti-monopoly Law Takes Effect" (2008) *Xinhua News Agency*

Owen B. M., Su Sun, Wentong Zheng, "China's Competition Policy Reforms: The Anti-monopoly Law and Beyond" (2008) *75 Antitrust L.J.* 231

Stucke, M. E., "Reconsidering Antitrust's Goals (2011) *Boston College Law Review*, Vol. 53, p. 551, 2012

Tian Yijun, "The Impacts of the Chinese Anti-Monopoly Law on IP Commercialization in China & General Strategies for Technology-Driven Companies and Future Regulators" (2010) *Duke Law & Technology Review*

Tsenchov, "Latest Development in the Microsoft Case in the European Union: Microsoft Officially Allows Browser Choice to Customers" (2010) *The Columbia Journal of European Law*, 16

Turney J., "Defining the Limits of the EU Essential Facilities Doctrine on Intellectual Property Rights: The Primacy of Securing Optimal Innovation" (2005) *Northwestern Journal of Technology and Intellectual Property*, Vol 3, No. 2.

Wang C., "Overview and Perspective of Civil Enforcement under the AML", *Competition Policy Research* (2016) March Issue

Wang X., "Highlights of China's New Anti-Monopoly Law" (2008) 75 *Antitrust L.J* 133, 144-46.

Wang X. "Preliminary observations and thoughts on China's first lawsuit concerning anti-monopoly law" (2006) *East Law Study*

Wu S., "China Publishes the 2nd Version of the Anti-Monopoly Guidelines on the Abuse of Intellectual Property Rights" (2017) *CPI Competition Policy International*

Zhang G. et al., "A Review of Huawei v. IDC", (2015) *Managing Intellectual Property*

Cases

China

Huawei v. InterDigital, Guangdong High People's Court, (2013)Yue Gao Fa Min San Zhong Zi No. 306

Watchdata System v. Hengbao Company, Ltd. (2015) Jing Zhi Min Chu Zi No.441

European Union

Bronner v. Mediaprint, C-7/97

Commercial Solvents v. Commission, C-7/73

Huawei Technologies Co. Ltd. v. ZTE Corp, ZTE Deutschland GmbH, C-170/13

Radio Telefis Eireann (RTE) and Independent Television Publications Ltd (ITP) v. Commission, Joined Cases C-241/91 P & C-242/91 P

Tetra Pak International v. Commission, C-333/94 P

US

Apple, Inc. v. Motorola Mobility, Inc. 886 F. Supp.2d 1061, 1067 (W.D. Wis. 2012)

Broadcom Corp. v. Qualcomm Inc., 501 F. 3d 297 (2007)

Microsoft Corporation v. Motorola, Inc., et al., C10-1823JLR (2012)

United States v. Terminal Railroad Association, 224 U.S. 383 (1912)

European Union Primary and Secondary Legislations

Commission Notice on Definition of Relevant Market

Commission Regulation (EU), 316/2014 on the application of Article 101(3) of the

Directive on certain rules governing actions for damages under national law for infringements of the competition law provisions of the Member States and of the European Union

Treaty on the Functioning of the European Union

Treaty on the Functioning of the European Union to categories of technology transfer agreement

Chinese Primary and Secondary Legislations

Anti-Monopoly Guidelines on the Abuse of Intellectual Property Rights (Draft for Comments)

Anti-Monopoly Law of the People's Republic of China

Anti-Unfair Competition Law of the People's Republic of China

Guidelines on Prohibition of Abuse of Intellectual Property Rights under the AML

Patent Law of the People's Republic of China

Price Law of the People's Republic of China

Provisions on Prohibition of Abuse of Intellectual Property Rights to Exclude and Restrict Competition

State Council Guideline on Definition of Relevant Market

Supreme People's Court Provision on the Application of Laws in Civil Disputes Cases Arising from Monopoly Activities

International Treaty

Agreement on Trade-Related Aspects of Intellectual Property Rights (TRIPS Agreement)

Other Sources

Administrative Sanction Decision from National Development and Reform Commission of People's Republic of China (2015), available at http://www.ndrc.gov.cn/gzdt/201503/t20150302_666209.html

Baron J. et al., "Essential Patent and Standard Dynamics", (2013), available at https://www.law.northwestern.edu/research-faculty/searlecenter/innovationeconomics/documents/Essential_Patents_and_Standard_Dynamics_2013.pdf

European Commission, *Report on Competition Policy 2010*, available at http://ec.europa.eu/competition/publications/annual_report/2010/part1_en.pdf

He L., et al, "Monopoly Dispute: Chinese Enterprise Won against American Giant" (2013) available at http://news.163.com/13/1028/21/9CA9N4JN00014JB6.html

InterDigital 10-Q report, filed October 31, 2013, available at http://www.snl.com/Cache/c34365872.html

Li, G. "Interface between International Property Rights and Competition Law – Implications of the Chinese Qualcomm Decision (2015)" (2017) *Seminar Paper* submitted to Prof. Josef Drexl in fulfillment of the request from MIPLC

Li H., "Rethinking the Competition Case, Huawei Wins the Lawsuit against IDC" (2015), available at http://www.maxlaw.cn/l/20150929/830281649635.shtml

Lin B., Jon Wood, Soonhee Jang, "Overview of Chinese Patent Law" (2004) 35th International Congress of the PIPA

Lipman M., "Antitrust Group Urges China to Adjust Approach to IP Abuse", Available at https://www.law360.com/articles/913654/antitrust-group-urges-china-to-adjust-approach-to-ip-abuse

Nie P., "China's First Anti-monopoly Law Takes Effect" (2008) Xinhua News Agency

Ohlhausen M. K., "Illuminating the Story of China's Anti-Monopoly Law" (2013), available at https://www.ftc.gov/sites/default/files/documents/public_statements/illuminating-story-chinas-anti-monopoly-law/1310amlstory.pdf

Pettinger T., "Criticism of IMF" (2012), available at http://www.economicshelp.org/blog/glossary/imf-criticism/

Pettinger T., "Washington Consensus – Definition and Criticism" (2013), available at

http://www.economicshelp.org/blog/7387/economics/washington-consensus-definition-and-criticism/

Slaughter and May, *Competition Law in China*, (2016) available at https://www.slaughterandmay.com/media/879862/competition-law-in-china.pdf

Stasik E., "Royalty Rates and Licensing Strategies for Essential Patents on LTE (4G) Telecommunication Standards" (2010) *Royalty rates for Telecommunications*

The World Bank, "Understanding China's Poverty Reduction Success to Benefit the Global South", available at http://www.worldbank.org/en/news/feature/2016/05/17/understanding-chinas-poverty-reduction-success-to-benefit-the-global-south

US Chamber of Commerce, "Competing interests in China's Competition Law Enforcement: China's Anti-Monopoly Law Application and the Role of Industrial Policy" (2014)

Wang P. J. et al., "New Chinese Anti-Monopoly Law" (2007), available at http://www.jonesday.com/New_Chinese_Anti-Monopoly_Law/

Wu S., "China Publishes the 2nd Version of the Anti-Monopoly Guidelines on the Abuse of Intellectual Property Rights" (2017) *CPI Competition Policy International*, available at https://www.competitionpolicyinternational.com/wp-content/uploads/2017/04/Asia-Column-April-Full.pdf